RETIRE LIKE A DAIRY FARMER

How to Never Outlive Your Money

EVAN HOOBCHAAK

BALBOA.
PRESS
A DIVISION OF HAY HOUSE

Balboa Press books may be ordered through booksellers or by contacting:

Balboa Press
A Division of Hay House
1663 Liberty Drive
Bloomington, IN 47403
www.balboapress.com
1 (877) 407-4847

Because of the dynamic nature of the Internet, any web addresses or links contained in this book may have changed since publication and may no longer be valid. The views expressed in this work are solely those of the author and do not necessarily reflect the views of the publisher, and the publisher hereby disclaims any responsibility for them.

This publication is designed to provide accurate and authoritative information in regard to the subject matter covered. It should be read with the understanding that the author is not engaged in rendering financial, legal, accounting, or other professional service.

The author of this book does not dispense medical advice or prescribe the use of any technique as a form of treatment for physical, emotional, or medical problems without the advice of a physician, either directly or indirectly. The intent of the author is only to offer information of a general nature to help you in your quest for emotional and spiritual well-being. In the event you use any of the information in this book for yourself, which is your constitutional right, the author and the publisher assume no responsibility for your actions.

Any people depicted in stock imagery provided by Getty Images are models, and such images are being used for illustrative purposes only.
Certain stock imagery © Getty Images.

Print information available on the last page.

ISBN: 978-1-4525-5816-5 (sc)
ISBN: 978-1-4525-5818-9 (hc)
ISBN: 978-1-4525-5817-2 (e)

Library of Congress Control Number: 2012916767

Balboa Press rev. date: 08/23/2019

DEDICATION

For my Mother and Father, who taught me to never
assume the accepted way is the best way.

CONTENTS

ACKNOWLEDGEMENTS

This book in its present format would not have been possible without the help of Alan Laduzinsky, Jill Steinberg, Karen Sandrick, and Scott Minnig. I'd also like to thank my wonderful wife, family, and colleagues, notably Joy Sweet and Larry Scattaglia, for their support.

The idea of retiring and supporting yourself tending to a small dairy farm in a bucolic setting, maintaining animals and selling produce at local markets may be appealing. I hope it's not the reason you're reading this book because **Retiring like a Dairy Farmer** is an analogy.

The life of the dairy farmer generally involves maintaining a herd of cows, keeping them healthy, and occasionally weeding out the sick and infirm. The goal is to use your cows for their milk which (since they are healthy cows) will be produced regularly and predictably.

Does the dairy farmer get up in the morning and, before doing anything else, frantically check the price of beef to see what his cows are worth if he were to sell or slaughter them? No, of course not. It would make no sense for a dairy farmer to worry about the daily price of beef. Instead, the dairy farmer instead gets up and milks the cows.

Instead of focusing on the value of your investment portfolio, look to the income it produces, which is easier to predict, control, and maintain.

By buying and maintaining a portfolio of income-producing investments (dairy cows), you can generate the distribution rate (milk) needed to support your lifestyle and not have to worry about what price the market places on your holdings. In addition, the "dairy farmer" approach to retirement income eliminates the fear of running out of money.

CHAPTER 1

Stop Worrying

The fear of running out of money in retirement dominates most conversations about retirement planning and investing. This angst often leads to decisions to work longer, spend less in retirement than you would like to, and invest retirement funds as conservatively as possible to avoid capital loss. Some may consider working longer, spending less, and investing conservatively as noble actions, but they are forced on retirees by market losses or the fear of market loss and take joy away from the retirement goal of lifelong workers.

Running out of money concerns investors because they (and their financial advisors) approach retirement income backwards. Rather than separating the distribution phase of investing from the accumulation phase, when it comes to portfolio growth they use the same assumptions for both – and this is where the income worries begin. The accumulation phase involves saving and investing for growth to build a nest egg to fund future goals. The distribution phase uses the nest egg for withdrawals. These are two very different stages of investment. The commonly used distribution approach is designed to reduce nest egg volatility and still invest for a measure of growth to offset any withdrawals.

Any investor who's been around for the past few decades knows the market can be very volatile and that relying on growth in any given year, even with an ultra-diversified portfolio, will cause anxiety. However, the idea that the only way to structure retirement investments for distribution is to rely on growth and sell off portions of the portfolio occasionally to raise cash remains a staple of mainstream financial advice.

The debate rages over what percentage of this growth-based "retirement portfolio" should be allocated to bonds, stocks, emerging markets, cash, gold, real estate, and so on, and how and when assets should be sold to raise cash. This misses the point because it's based on the assumption that you need to hope your retirement assets grow to avoid running out of money.

This continued focus on investing retirement portfolio for growth is based on the research of Bill Bengen, an MIT-educated Certified Financial Planner Practitioner ™. In an article published in the **Journal for Financial Planning** in the 1990s, Bengen wrote that, based on decades of back-tested market data, one could safely withdraw up to 4% of a portfolio and have a very good chance of that portfolio lasting one's lifetime.[1] Recent research shows that the ideal withdrawal rate may be even less because of the current low interest rate environment. In any case, this idea of a "magic" withdrawal rate has taken off and is still used as the benchmark for retirement income planning.

The "Magic Withdrawal Rate" approach relies on market growth. If you want to slowly deplete your retirement assets and hope (the key word being *hope*) your portfolio experiences market gain more often than it experiences market loss, then the Bengen model is for you. If you like to worry about a rising or declining market affecting depletion of your nest egg, go with the Bengen approach. However, research shows that retiring in a bear market versus retiring into a bull market greatly affects whether a retiree will run out of money. And we would all like to think we can identify market tops and market bottoms, but timing a market is difficult and only introduces anxiety.

Bengen and his "magic withdrawal rate" is not wrong. His approach to retirement income is just misguided. It's like attempting to open a closed door that you mistakenly assume is locked. You kick and shoulder the door, when all you have to do is turn the handle. When you start with the wrong assumptions (that assets must be sold to provide retirement income), it doesn't matter how you work to solve the problem.

Let's change the focus from growth or depletion of assets to *maintaining* them. You can have a withdrawal rate of 4.5% – or 5.5%, for that matter – and not have to worry about selling assets and running out of money.

CHAPTER 2

Envision your Retirement

Before we jump into a discussion about structuring a portfolio for retirement income, there are several key steps that everyone who is considering retirement must complete. Skip these steps and you invite unneeded risk and doubt into the next 30 to 40 years of your life.

The first step is to have an idea of what your retirement might look like. This includes dreams as well as realities, like healthcare. Retirement isn't what it used to be and may require continued employment, ideally doing something that provides enjoyment or just reduced time at your current job. Hobbies, volunteer work, and recreational activities can easily replace hours spent at a full-time job as well. It doesn't matter what your retirement looks like, as long as you are retiring to something.

Give a lot of thought to the social circles you'll be a part of once you're retired. If you're retiring to escape something – a boss, a monotonous job, or co-workers – you'll find yourself bored and disenchanted with retirement. It's easy to underestimate the value of the social network you're a part of while you're working. In some cases, you'll have spent time with the same people several times a week for decades. While you may not consider them friends *per se*, they've played an active role in your social life. Planning for this is critical to avoid missing going to work. We are all human, after all, and require a degree of social interaction.

An important aspect of setting up your "retire to something" proposition is what step one is about: thinking about the activities you want to pursue. These could be as simple as reading more books and spending time with grandchildren to planning your around-the-world vacations. In either case, these activities will directly influence your lifestyle expenses in retirement.

Step two is to put a price tag on your retirement vision. I believe that the mainstream financial media idea about retirement expenses automatically reducing to 80% of your pre-retirement level is nonsense. Why would you want to live at a reduced lifestyle once you're retired? That sounds like no fun. What I've seen is a tendency for lifestyle expenses to *increase* (in the 110% to 120% range of your lifestyle while working) for at least the first decade or two of retirement. After all, most people who are liberated from their jobs don't want to sit around and watch the "Price is Right" all day. While you're younger, healthy, and able-bodied you probably want to travel, dine out, and enjoy life to a degree that you weren't afforded when you were busy working 40-plus hours a week. Naturally, this enjoyment will translate into an increased cost of living. Further down the road and typically into your mid-80s, you may see your lifestyle expenses come down as you may travel less. However, healthcare costs may in fact replace the difference; all the more reason to plan on an inflated cost of living.

How much will you need to retire?

While ranges of income are helpful, it's ultimately up to you to sit down and track your spending habits. The retirement process shouldn't be just about budgeting. By simply tracking your pre-retirement expenses, you'll have a very good idea of what you'll spend in retirement by adding activities like additional travel, dining out, and recreation. Knowing exactly what your monthly expenses amount to is critical. This number will dictate the distribution rate needed from your investment portfolio. After taking into account all fixed income sources such as a pension and social security, or a deferred compensation plan, the difference between your expenses and fixed income sources will need to be made up. Here's a quick worksheet to better illustrate the breakdown:

Retirement Income Sources:
- o Social Security =   _____
- o + Pension/Deferred Compensation =   _____
- o + Earned Income =   _____
- o + Passive/Rental Income =   _____
- o + Any Additional Income =   _____
  - § **Total Income =**   _____

Retirement Lifestyle Expenses:
- o Mortgage / Rent payments =   _____
- o + Real Estate Taxes =   _____
- o + Utilities =   _____
- o + Home/Renter's and Auto Insurance =   _____
- o + Home Maintenance / Improvement =   _____
- o + Groceries =   _____
- o + Dining Out =   _____
- o + Clothing =   _____
- o + Auto Payments* =   _____
- o + Auto Fuel/Maintenance =   _____
- o + Insurance premiums
     (life, health, long-term care) =   _____
- o + Medical / Dental / Prescription costs =   _____
- o + Telephone / Mobile =   _____
- o + Cable / Internet =   _____
- o + Member Dues =   _____
- o + Hobbies / Recreation =   _____
- o + Travel =   _____
- o + Gifts =   _____
- o o + Pets =   _____
- o o + Support of Parents and/or Children   _____
- o + Charitable Donations =   _____
- o + Personal Care (haircuts, spa, etc.) =   _____
- o + Miscellaneous =   _____
  - § **Total Expenses =**   _____

*Assume some auto payments. Even if your current vehicles are paid off, eventually they'll need to be replaced. Ideally, the amount you allocate here, if not needed to pay a current car payment, should be saved into a cash account so that the down payment (or entire cost of a new car) will be available to you without causing cash flow issues.

Right about now you may be thinking, "There's no way I'm going to start tracking everything I spend or budgeting myself." The good news is, you don't have to. In fact, I find it tedious myself and I suggest the following shortcut. Since it's really not important to understand where the money is being spent (unless you feel you may be over-spending in a particular area or you're just curious), by simply aggregating bills from your commonly used debit or credit cards with anything paid in cash or by check, you should have quite an accurate number for your total lifestyle expenses. Even easier, let online and computer programs such as **Mint.com** and Quicken do a lot of the work for you.

Once you've got a clear picture of your income and expenses, the only other item you'll need is total assets that you have dedicated to retirement. Your 401(k), 403(b), 457, profit-sharing, IRA, Roth IRA, and annuity assets fall into this category. Any funds set aside in non-qualified (non-retirement-specific accounts) brokerage accounts or direct investment should be included.

Depending on your situation, cash value in life insurance policies could also be included in the retirement asset category. I would refrain from including cash reserve assets (such as checking, savings, and money market accounts) unless you plan on investing a portion of them for retirement income. You'll always want a cash buffer between you and unexpected expenses or purchases. This quick worksheet will help you aggregate your retirement accounts.

Investable Retirement Assets:
- o 401(k)/403(b)/457/Profit Sharing = _____
- o + IRA = _____
- o + Roth IRA = _____
- o + Non-Qualified Investment accounts = _____
- o + Annuity = _____

Possibly Included:

- o + Life Insurance Cash Value = _____
- o + Un-invested Cash above 6-12 months
    of expenses = _____
    § **Total Retirement Assets Available =** _____

From here, the calculation goes like this. Say your total after tax annual expenses come to around $110,000 including everything, and your total fixed retirement income totals $40,000. The income gap, or what will need to be made up from your investments, will come to $70,000 per year. To find your distribution rate, divide the $70,000 figure into the total amount of retirement specific assets. If we assume you have $1,500,000 in retirement-specific assets, your distribution rate is 4.67% (70,000 / 1,500,000). Put a little more cleanly:

Total Income = $40,000
minus
Total Expenses = $110,000
equals
Deficit / Surplus = -$70,000

$70,000 / $1,500,000 = 4.67% Distribution Rate Required

Already, you're above the magic 4.5%. However, a 4.67% distribution rate should be nothing to worry about when you treat your retirement investments like dairy cows.

Here's another example that dispels the myth of having to be a millionaire in order to comfortably retire. Your after tax annual expenses come to a total of $60,000 ($5,000 per month), which is a comfortable and enjoyable lifestyle for many, and fixed retirement income totals $45,000. The gap of $15,000 per year would need to be produced by retirement assets. Even a modest $300,000 portfolio invested for a 5% distribution rate would cover the $15,000 income gap. Again, put more cleanly:

Total Income ($45,000) minus *Total Expenses = ($60,000)* equals
Deficit / Surplus = -$15,000

$15,000 / $300,000 = 5% Distribution Rate Required

The lesson from this example is that you may not need as much as you think to live comfortably in retirement. Many retirees assume that since they'll never have a $1,000,000 or larger retirement account, retirement won't be as enjoyable as they'd like.

Controlling expenses in retirement by having a mortgage paid off or by budgeting where possible can be very important in making your retirement assets go as far as possible. Furthermore, going through the expense-tracking exercise in detail may surprise you. Don't assume you'll need to replace your current salary to retire effectively. After pre-tax savings and taxes are taken out, a gross salary may result in a net of 50% to 75% of the amount. A $100,000 pre-retirement salary may very well translate into a $60,000 lifestyle, making the expense-tracking exercise a very individual and important step.

In the next chapters, I'll cover how to produce the distribution rate you need to make up this income deficit, without having to worry about running out of money. Before we get there, though, I want to cover the commonly misunderstood retirement income source that is Social Security. Knowing a few tricks here could lower your distribution rate by possibly increasing one of your fixed income sources.

CHAPTER 3

Maximizing Social Security

Approximately 90% of retirees age 65 and older receive monthly Social Security benefits[2]. The understanding that Social Security income will most likely be a part (whether large or small) of your retirement lifestyle is fairly straightforward. However, knowing exactly when you should start receiving your Social Security benefits isn't so simple. While each situation is different, I hope to outline some broad guidelines that you can go by as well as explain some little known Social Security retirement benefit rules that you may be able to use.

"When should I start receiving Social Security benefits?" is one of the most commonly asked questions by retirees. There are two basic schools of thought on the issue – one essentially being the sooner the better, the other being the longer you wait before taking benefits, the more money you'll receive over your lifetime.

The exact answer would be very easy to calculate if you only knew how long you're going to live. If you knew you were going to die at age 65, taking Social Security benefits at age 62 (the earliest possible age at which retirement benefits can be taken) would be a no-brainer. If you knew you were going to live until you were 95 years old, it may make more sense to defer your benefits until age 70 because the amount of Social Security you will receive increases each year that you don't take the benefits. The fear of dying young often leads people to take benefits early, their thought being, "Might as well make sure I at least get *something*." While the logic certainly makes sense, make sure you consider the following strategies before jumping to elect benefits as soon as you are eligible.

First, if you plan on earning some income once you retire, pay careful attention to the earned income limits pertaining to Social Security benefits prior to your full retirement age. The following chart from the Social Security Administration's website (http://ssa.gov) shows you the age at which you can receive full retirement benefits:

Age To Receive Full Social Security Benefits	
Year of Birth	Full Retirement Age
1937 or earlier	65
1938	65 and 2 months
1939	65 and 4 months
1940	65 and 6 months
1941	65 and 8 months
1942	65 and 10 months
1943--1954	66
1955	66 and 2 months
1956	66 and 4 months
1957	66 and 6 months
1958	66 and 8 months
1959	66 and 10 months
1960 and later	67 [3]

Prior to this age and beginning the first full month that you reach age 62, you may elect to receive your Social Security retirement benefits. However, and this is important to understand, not only will your lifetime benefit be permanently reduced because you took benefits early, but you may lose out on benefits altogether if you continue to earn income.

In 2019, the annual earned income limit was $17,640 for those receiving Social Security benefits prior to the year in which they reach full retirement age. For every $2 earned above the limit, your Social Security benefits will actually be reduced by $1. Not taxed, mind you, *reduced*. So, in addition to permanently reducing your benefits throughout your lifetime, you won't be actually receiving current benefits if you continue earning more than the prescribed limits. As a general rule, if you plan on earning above the income limits prior to your full retirement age, consider waiting to take Social Security.

Besides the earned income limit pitfall prior to full retirement age, you may want to consider waiting to receive benefits even after you have reached full retirement age. That is because the Social Security Administration will boost your benefit for each month that it is not taken. For those born in 1943 and later, the delayed retirement credit is 8% per year – certainly not a bad return for any investment, let alone a fixed income source.

If you absolutely need Social Security income to support yourself in retirement, then you may not have flexibility when it comes to delaying election of your benefits. However, if you don't mind working another year or two or pulling money from other sources for a few years, taking advantage of the 8% delayed retirement credit may make sense. You'll simply be increasing the "milk" coming out of the government cow.

For married couples, the delayed retirement credit can be especially powerful in that it permanently increases widow benefits as well. So, for a couple with one person as the main wage earner, that person will earn an 8% return by waiting to receive benefits past their full retirement age. This also will increase the surviving spouse's income. While we tend to not like to focus on what will happen when we're gone, ensuring greater retirement income for a spouse may be an important consideration when waiting to elect Social Security retirement benefits.

Spousal Social Security Benefits

Due to changes made to Social Security in 2015, many assume that spousal benefits are no longer a filing option. While the "File and Suspend" strategy has been eliminated for those born after January 2nd, 1954, there are still clever ways to maximize your Social Security benefits via Spouse's benefits.

As long as your spouse has been married to you for at least one year, he or she may claim a retirement benefit based on the relationship to you. Essentially, the spouse is entitled to 50% of the main wage earner's full retirement benefit at the spouse's full retirement age. If non-working spouses simply assume that they aren't eligible for Social Security benefits, they could be leaving significant dollars on the table.

Furthermore, claiming a spouse's benefit doesn't affect or reduce in any way the main wage earner's retirement benefit. Even non-married individuals may be able to take advantage of these benefits. A divorced, and not remarried, spouse (age 62 or older) is eligible to elect spouse's benefits based on the ex's earnings record as long as they were married for at least 10 years.

Because a spouse's benefits don't affect the retirement benefits of the person they're connected to, the divorced spouse doesn't need to worry about contacting their ex regarding the spouse's benefit. As long as the proper documentation exists (marriage certificate, divorce decree, proper identification, etc.) a local Social Security Administration office should be able to track down benefits and deem who is eligible to receive what.

When an age difference exists between two spouses, incorporating spousal benefits into the filing strategy can be particularly powerful. For example, take a retired married couple, Dan and Sue, who are ages 66 and 62. Dan's Full Retirement Age benefit from Social Security is $2,788 and Sue' FRA benefit is $977 due to wage differences over the course of their lifetimes. The common filing strategy would involve Dan taking his retirement benefit and Sue taking the spousal benefit off of that amount since it would be higher than her own retirement benefit. While this maximizes the near-term dollar amount available to Dan and Sue from the Social Security Administration, it can leave money on the table by completely ignoring Sue's own retirement benefit.

By flipping the filing strategy around and still using spousal benefits, Dan and Sue can better maximize cash flow over their lifetimes. In this scenario, Sue would file for her retirement benefit of $712 at age 62 and Dan would claim spousal benefits of $489 immediately as he is 66 years old. This strategy brings in over $1,200 per month right away and allows Dan's retirement benefit to continue to compound at 8%. When Dan reaches age 70, he will switch to his retirement benefit which will then have grown to $3,680 and Sue will take spousal benefits resulting in a payment to her of $1,106.

While less money is available from Social Security right away by having Sue file for her retirement benefits and Dan file for spousal benefits, the total amount received over time (assuming a normal life expectancy) is greatly increased. Locking in a higher guaranteed lifetime income stream by maximizing Social Security spousal benefit strategies can have a significant impact on retirement cash flow as well as provide a type of longevity insurance by ensuring maximum retirement benefits are claimed. In fact, it can make sense in certain situations to pull extra from savings or investment accounts for a few years to help out cash flow while allowing Social Security to compound via spousal benefit claiming strategies.

We're now dealing with assumptions about life and death that may not be accurate in the end. But in some cases, knowing the effects of delaying versus receiving benefits and how to best take advantage of spouse's benefits may result in hundreds of thousands of additional dollars in benefits over one's lifetime.

14

Changing your mind

Finally, if you've already elected to receive benefits but realize that it may have made more sense to wait, the Social Security Administration *does* allow you to change your mind. Once in your lifetime and no more than 12 months after you have decided to take retirement benefits, you may contact the Social Security Administration and request to reapply. In order for your request to be accepted, you will be required to repay all benefits including taxes and any Medicare premiums withheld from your benefits. However, no interest will be charged, so it's not that costly of a mistake as long as the funds are available to repay the benefits received.

While I don't want to confuse you with the intricacies of Social Security retirement benefits, I do want to emphasize the importance of giving your Social Security benefits some thought before electing them as well as making sure you take advantage of the rules regarding spouse's benefits, earned income limitations, delayed retirement credits, etc. Rather than simply electing benefits because you can or retiring at a specific "full retirement age" because "Social Security says I should be retired," make sure you review the long-term impact and timing of electing your Social Security retirement benefits as it may mean more money in your pocket.

CHAPTER 4

The Dairy Farmer Approach To Investing

We have reviewed how to determine your retirement income, expenses, and distribution rate from your investments as well as gleaned some tips to potentially maximize your social security benefits. I want to get back to the actual setup of your "dairy cow" portfolio. I will approach the subject with three different questions in mind: Why?, How?, and When?

I won't describe a hypothetical portfolio but instead will dig deep into the arguments for this income-oriented approach. I will also show you at what age such a portfolio should be considered. Understanding all three questions will help you grasp what retiring like a dairy farmer really means for your peace of mind both leading up to and living through retirement.

Why Be A Dairy Farmer Investor?

Why? The metaphor of treating your investments like a dairy farmer treats his cows is about simplicity. Using distribution yield (the amount of income produced by your investments in relation to the overall portfolio total) rather than hoping for growth takes almost all of the anxiety out of investing. Instead of worrying about factors completely outside of your control (like market price movements) you can focus on the more predictable and stable income production.

Some good examples of this approach are showcased by 3M Co. common stock (MMM) and a 10-year U.S. government bond. Both investments, while very different in nature (stock vs. bond), could be characterized as "dairy cows" because they can produce stable and predictable streams of income.

You can go to the 3M Co.'s investor website and find the historical dividend information very easily. Looking through the information will show you that 3M Co. has paid a dividend every quarter for the last 380 quarters (95 years) and has increased the dividend consecutively for 53 years.[4] That's almost a century of consistent "milk" received for the dairy farmer investor. Over that same time period, by the way, the stock price of 3M Co. has gone up and down without much predictability.

Investing like a dairy farmer comes down to this simple question: "Would you rather bet on 3M Co. paying dividends next year or 3M Co. stock posting a gain?" The first relies on not much more than 3M Co. continuing to operate as a business while the second involves so many other factors related to the global market psychology that it's mind-boggling.

The idea is the same with the 10-year U.S. Government Treasury bond. Are you comfortable betting on the U.S. government? Will it continue to pay its debtors or do you want to bet on interest rate fluctuations due to global "flight to safety" trades or the Federal Reserve actions?

While recent political events have raised the real question of whether or not the U.S. government will pay its debts, the fact remains that it is much easier to predict an ongoing income stream than day-to-day or even year-to-year price movements.

When it comes to income streams, I don't know if 3M Co. common stock or a 10-year Treasury bond will always be so predictable. But when you diversify a retirement portfolio across multiple asset classes and holdings and focus on income stability and predictability rather than on whether the investment will go up or down, you set yourself up for success in producing the necessary distribution rate to fund your retirement lifestyle.

Predictability

What does *predictable* mean?. Sure, at any time 3M could choose to reduce or stop paying the quarterly dividend. However, given the company's 95-year commitment to the dividend policy, it's not very likely. Could the U.S. government stop making interest payments on its debt and default? Certainly, but again, it's not very likely.

These risks to income are much less when compared to the risk of market loss. Where you're taking risk is what's most important, not the idea of risk itself. Are you risking your retirement on whether 3M Co.'s stock price rises or falls or whether 3M continues to pay you a dividend? Are you risking your retirement on whether interest rates rise or fall or whether the U.S. government continues to pay interest on its debt? Essentially, the simplicity of the approach comes from setting a much lower hurdle for your investments to clear.

No more relying on market-driven price movements

You need to separate the concept of dividend and interest income from price fluctuations Understanding this concept alone allows you to become a better investor. When it comes to picking any investment, it's easy to get caught up in the "buy low, sell high" principle, which is what we are all essentially told to follow as we begin to invest. However, just like the dairy farmer focusing only on milk production, so should you as a retirement investor focus only on income production.

Whether you sell cows or investments $10 higher or lower ultimately shouldn't matter much if you can still meet the end goal of milk or income production. Also, as long as you continue to meet this end goal of income years out from the initial purchase, whether the prices of the investments have gone up or down shouldn't matter.

Psychologically, we all like to see an increase in an investment's value. But for the investor focused on distribution yield, if the income produced from the investment remains the same, it doesn't matter what the price action is. These two charts help illustrate this point:

3M CO. (MMM)   WEEKLY PRICE

ROLLING DIVIDENDS

The top chart plots the stock price of 3M Co. shares over a 5-year period, from roughly 2007 to 2012, and the bottom chart plots the dividend in cents per share over the same time period. The investor focused on growth and the investor focused on income have very different experiences over those 5 years. While both owned the same stock and experienced the same events – including price dips, stock price rallies, and dividend payouts – the two might have a very different opinion of the last 5 years as a 3M Co. shareholder.

The investor who is focused on growth might say, "Boy, that 3M stock is such a dog. I bought it 5 years ago around $80 and it's still at the same price. And along the way it sure took me on a roller coaster ride. There were some sleepless nights in early 2009 when I was down almost 50%."

The investor who is focused on income and distribution yield might have a completely different viewpoint: "That 3M stock is great. Five years ago it was paying me just under $0.50 per share. Now it's *not only still paying me, but the stock is paying me 10% more.* Plus, I still have the same amount of money I originally invested. What a great deal!"

Same stock, same time period, two completely different experiences. For the retired investor hoping for stock price increases and growth as a way to maintain their retirement portfolio and support their lifestyle, 3M Co. common stock was a complete letdown. For the retired investor treating their investments like dairy cows and focusing solely on distribution yield, 3M Co. stock was a complete success.

Not only did the dividend continue through the worst recession in generations, it actually increased, providing more and more income each year. 3M Co. common stock isn't an exception either. If you include other asset classes like bonds and preferred stocks, there are hundreds, if not thousands, of examples that provided the same type of experience during that 5-year period.

Just focusing on distribution yield sounds easy enough, but it is critically important to remember that both the growth investor and the income investor held the stock continuously for the 5-year period. In both of our examples, neither investor panicked and sold their shares when things got really bad.

However, there are plenty of us out there who would have given up when the stock was down 50% and sold. That's why it is so important to divorce the concept of pricing from that of income production. Both investors' statements would have been equally as ugly in early 2009, showing a 50% loss.

The dairy farmer investor would focus on the end goal of income production and talked his or herself off of the ledge, saying, "While the market is telling me my investment in 3M Co. is worth half of what it was a few years ago, the dividend has actually increased, the company is still healthy, and the outlook is for the dividend to continue. Why would I want to sell the stock?"

You could see an actual dairy farmer having a similar thought process when it comes to a particular cow: "If I took that cow to market to sell her, I would get only half of what I would have gotten a few years ago, but she's still producing as much milk as she was then if not more and looks healthy as ever."

"Who cares what someone else tells me she's worth. I only care about the milk and from that point of view, she's just fine." Further on in the book, I'll cover specific situations when *it* is time to sell off of a dairy cow investment, but for our purposes of understanding the concept of separating price from income, this is a great example.

A portfolio you can't outlive

In addition to focusing on distribution yield, there are additional reasons why the dairy farmer approach to investing makes so much sense.

The ultimate goal is to create a predictable and stable income stream from your investments through a simple and repeatable process. Then you won't worry every time the market drops.

The dairy farmer approach also creates an income-producing portfolio that you can't outlive. Simple logic dictates that taking only dividend and interest income from a portfolio maintains its value. You should still have access to the same principal even 50 or 60 years into the future.

The retired investor living only on the income produced by their portfolio would still have access to the same (if not substantially more) dollars at any point in the future. While there are times where the principal value will drop (2008-2009, for example), the long-term trend of the stock market is up. Bonds, if held to maturity, will return the same amount of principal invested.

I've heard the response, "I don't have any heirs and I certainly don't want to leave a single dollar behind when I go." There's nothing wrong with not leaving an inheritance, but unless you know the exact day you'll die or what your exact health care, long-term care, or hospice expenses are going to be, it's foolish to think you could perfectly deplete your investment portfolio to naught on the day you die.

The dairy farmer approach innately preserves principal for the unknown and unforeseen. By focusing on distribution yield, a retired investor can create a perpetual income stream but still be allowed access to the underlying principal amount. Furthermore, if left untouched, the underlying principal should increase over time. It would be very rare for a portfolio to deliver negative capital returns over a 20+ year time frame.

Protecting purchasing power

An often-overlooked benefit to the distribution yield investment approach is that it protects purchasing power.

Inflation is the stealthiest threat to a retired investor. It never shows itself on a quarterly statement, nor will it announce itself like a dividend cut or bond default.

The overly conservative investor who is focused only on principal preservation will see income and principal slowly erode because of inflation.

The lesson here is not to run away from "market risk" that results from the daily fluctuations of global stock markets. Treating your investments like dairy cows allows you to do this. Just realize that the alternative of sitting in risk-free conservative investments will not lead to success in the long run because of inflation.

Evan iIf you're fortunate enough to have enough investment principal where even a 1-2% distribution yield will produce the income necessary for your retirement lifestyle, don't be fooled into thinking you can park the money in a guaranteed money market account or Certificate of Deposit.

You may not notice the effect of inflation for 5, even 10 years, and you may even be proud of yourself for being immune from the ups and downs of the stock market. But, think back to the price of a postage stamp, gallon of gas, loaf of bread, pound of beef, or gallon of milk 10 years ago.

Setting up a portfolio to produce the desired distribution yield today is important. It's even more important to ensure the purchasing power of the income produced by that portfolio. One dollar today won't have the same purchasing power in 10 years, let alone 20 or 30 years. A high yielding bond will pay the same amount for its duration, never increasing the income it pays you regardless of what level of inflation you're experiencing with your lifestyle expenses.

With money market accounts, Certificates of Deposit, and even bonds, you're at the mercy of interest rates in terms of if and when your interest income will increase. Often, risk-free interest rates significantly lag behind the true rate of inflation. But certain dividend-paying stocks have consistent track records of providing regular increases to the dividend that can offset purchasing power erosion.

Dividend-paying stocks are a unique form of inflation protection. Their value is typically tied to a company that sells goods or services in a particular currency. If inflation and the costs of operation for the company are rising, the company will raise its prices. This price increase will translate into higher revenues, higher earnings per share, and higher cash flow. This, in turn, usually translates into an increased dividend.

While not perfect, this strategy allows the investor who allocates a significant portion of their income-producing investments to dividend-paying stocks to fare much better in an inflationary environment than an investor who relies on fixed-income investments.

You may say, "That's fine when I can only earn 1% in a guaranteed investment, but what if I can get a long-term triple AAA bond paying 5%? Why wouldn't I just pour my money into that, get my 5% for life, and not worry about any stock risk at all?"

Again, looking into the future 10, 15, or 20 years, you have to realize that the 5% distribution rate from that bond will never change. Regardless of the dollar amount invested, the 5% bond will always produce the same income because a fixed coupon bond doesn't increase its payout. Over time, the loss of purchasing power will reduce that 5% payout in real terms.

Your "dairy cow" type of dividend-paying stocks are one of the few investments that protect the purchasing power of your retirement dollars long into the future. Purchasing power protection and principal maintenance are concrete reasons for adopting the dairy farmer approach to investing.

Emerging Trends

The next few rationales to help understand the "why" of investing like a dairy farmer are more educated guesses about what investors may see moving forward. Relying solely on historical precedent and backward-looking data can be a recipe for disaster. The next two emerging trends, I believe, will further the need for a distribution yield focused approach to retirement investing more so than ever before.

Interest rates

Since about 1980, interest rates have moved in a steady and slow decline from the high teens to the low single digits or practically zero depending on the metrics you look at. A bond's yield (the amount of interest it pays) moves inversely to its price. So, in a falling interest rate environment, all other things being equal, a bond's price will increase.

In a rising interest rate environment, all other things being equal, a bond's price will decrease. (Without getting too detailed, the relationship works this way because a bond paying a certain interest rate is worth more if prevailing rates have subsequently fallen, making the higher income stream generated by the higher interest rate bond that much more valuable.)

On the flip side, a lower interest rate bond will be worth less if an investor can go buy a bond paying a higher income stream. That is, how much more valuable is the bond you bought that pays 3% when someone else could only buy a new bond that pays 2%. Conversely, how much less valuable is a bond paying 2% worth if someone can buy a new bond at 3%.

This relationship has made it very easy for investors in almost any type of bond to make handsome returns over the last 35 years. Because prevailing interest rates kept falling save for a few blips up here and there, the price of almost any bond bought between 1980 and 2010 increased.

Bond returns became not only a function of the income they paid, but also had a significant capital appreciation component factored in over this time period. On the surface, this doesn't seem like a problem at all. So what if bond investors over the past 30 to 35 years made out really well, earning income as well as watching the value of their bonds increase.

The problem lies in the assumption that these returns will continue for the next 30 to 35 years. What if the 7%-9% average annual returns over the past 35 years[5] in bonds become 1-3% average annual returns? How will that affect overall portfolio return assumptions? For the growth-focused investor, this presents a serious problem.

While interest rates could stay low or perhaps fall even lower (unlikely since we're already close to 0%), it is reasonable to expect a rising interest rate cycle at some point in the near future. As this chart indicates, interest rates have a long history of moving in distinct cycles. I did mention earlier that it is dangerous to extrapolate historical trends, however, we should at least be aware of the cyclical nature of interest rates. Interest rates most likely won't go sky-high anytime soon, but even modest increases in interest rates can lead to reduced returns and potential losses.

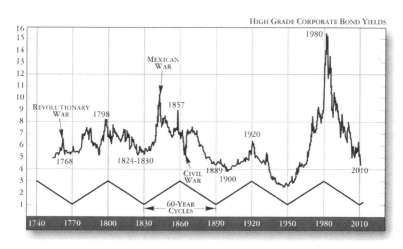

Benefits of owning individual bonds

Current bond holders will have an uphill battle if interest rates start climbing as the bond price increases that buoyed bond returns in a falling interest rate environment will suddenly become bond price decreases. Even if you own a bond paying 5% per year in income, if that bond loses a few percent due to prevailing market interest rates increasing, your total return will suffer mightily.

A good way to combat the effects of rising rates is not to stop investing in bonds, but to make sure you own bonds in the right way. Treat them like dairy cows and own bonds for income, not total return, but also own them individually rather than through mutual funds.

Why go through the tedium of selecting and buying bonds individually rather than through a fund? It comes down to controlling the maturity date of the bonds you own – to have a set date in the future when you know you will be getting your money back, regardless of what interest rates have done.

Common stocks don't have a fixed value and can trade for essentially any value someone thinks they're worth. Bonds give the income investor the advantage of knowing the value of a current income stream as well as what the value of the investment will be years into the future.

An investor who owns $1,000 worth of a bond maturing in 2020 can expect to get exactly $1,000 back in 2020, barring a bankruptcy or default of the underlying entity. That same bond's price may move up or down from now until 2020 depending on prevailing interest rates.

But the investor can at least be assured of getting their money back to reinvest into another investment. That's why it's worth owning the individual bonds.

In a mutual fund, bonds are constantly being bought and sold and there's no set maturity date or value that you can expect to receive at any date in the future. You just have to hope that the bond mutual fund can weather a rising interest rate cycle and not lose too much of your principal value. If it were up to me, I would like the certainty of knowing exactly how much my bond investment is worth at a specific date in the future.

Rising rates will eventually benefit the income investor as bond yields will rise with rates and ultimately make them more attractive investments from an income point of view. In the worst-case scenario, if you control the maturity dates of your bonds, you will always be able to reinvest the bond proceeds into a higher interest rate investment if rates have risen.

Most investors haven't seen a multi-decade cycle of rising rates and what that can do to the total return of bond investments. If you focus on the income stream and directly control the maturity date by owning individual bonds, you should be able to use the relative safety of bonds but still effectively preserve capital, produce income, and weather a much more difficult environment for bond investors moving forward.

Fat tails

An unfortunate emerging trend in the markets that makes it all the more important to treat your investments like dairy cows is the concept of "fat tails."[6] If you think of a typical bell curve, starting from the bottom left, swooping up to the middle and then falling again to the bottom right, the far left and far right of the curve illustrate the remote chances of an extreme condition occurring. The vast majority of events described by the bell curve will fall somewhere in the middle.

What the markets have increasingly shown us is that the "once-in-a-lifetime" events aren't so rare. What the fat-tail concept tries to explain is that the bell curve, when applied to the market, should be much flatter, with the far left and far right tails encompassing far more possible outcomes.

While it's impossible to identify the exact reasons for the increased volatility, some of it may lie in the globalization of trading markets and the relatively new phenomenon of "flash trading." The globalization of these markets has led to many benefits, the largest being the increased liquidity for all investors. With many more buyers and sellers across the globe using computers and the Internet to move money, the overall ability of an investor to buy or sell at a particular time at a more efficient price has increased.

Flash trading takes this principle to a higher level. It essentially exploits the thousandths-of-a-penny difference that can exist between buyer's bids and seller's asking prices across the globe with algorithm-led trades that can fire off multiple orders every second. Again, the benefit is increased liquidity for everyone, but with computer algorithms in control across trading systems, things can go awry.

A great example is the "Flash Crash" of May 2010.[7] The exact cause may never be known, but within about an hour on May 6, 2010, the market plunged around 9% but recovered most of those losses by the end of the trading day.

Some individual stocks like Procter & Gamble (PG), a usually boring stock when it comes to intra-day movements, fell more than 50% for a period of time. What caused the huge drops in the absence of any major news event or root cause is suspected to be the cascading of sell orders that algorithm-based trading systems activated at the same time.

The quick recovery of the losses points to an "electronic" mistake. While some steps have been put in place to hopefully prevent such a drop again, it is a good assumption for the investor to make that as long as algorithm-led trading exists, the risk of a huge drop is ever-present.

Regardless the reasons for increased volatility, what this means for the investor is that average returns may stay roughly the same, but 30%, 40%, and even 50% moves may become more commonplace – sometimes within one day! For someone who is relying on growth to get by in retirement, going through that type of roller coaster ride may not be an ideal experience.

What's more dangerous is what happens to a distribution rate when subjected to severe market swings. A growth focused investor with a conservative 4% distribution rate sees their distribution rate jump to 8% in a prolonged 50% market decline. An 8% distribution rate simply isn't sustainable and now, because of uncontrollable market events, a retirement portfolio may end up getting depleted much more quickly than expected.

Essentially, the growth focused investor has to hope the market comes back quickly to help lower the distribution rate. As described earlier, a dairy farmer investor going through that same market experience wouldn't have much to worry about as the distribution rate is based solely on income being produced by the investments.

Even though the market will fall just as much for the dairy farmer investor as for the growth focused investor, the different expectations for the investment portfolios and the income derived from these portfolios make all the difference. As long as dividends and income continue to be paid, even a 50% market decline will not change the lifestyle of a dairy farmer investor.

This control and the simplicity behind this type of distribution yield focused approach should convince anyone approaching retirement (or currently retired) to overhaul current assumptions regarding how to build a portfolio. Retirement and the years leading up to it shouldn't be fraught with worries of a market collapse.

Investing like a dairy farmer should allow your response to the question, "What did the market do today?" to always be, "It doesn't matter to me."

CHAPTER 5

Components of the Dairy Farmer Approach

Now that you understand the thought process behind investing like a dairy farmer, I want to walk you through the process of selecting dairy cow investments. In the chapters to come, I will present specific portfolio allocations with investment examples selected. The intent is to demonstrate how to properly build a portfolio focused on distribution yield from the ground up by evaluating the individual investment classes and examples within each class.

There are five key components that need to be part of any distribution yield focused income portfolio:

1. Safe reserve
2. Maturity date controlled fixed income portfolio
3. Dividend superstars
4. Alternative income producers
5. High income (but not necessarily high risk)

This chapter will cover the first two components, with chapters 6, 7, and 8 covering the next three.

Creating a safe reserve

The "safe reserve" is a non-income producing conservative growth investment mix that you may need to access no matter how well you plan. We are all presented with unforeseen expenses as well as opportunities in our lives. Having a portion of even your "investable" monies allocated to a safe haven is important for this reason. It is easy to fall into the mindset of, "If I allocated these dollars to the other income-producing investments, I'd have that much more money to spend in retirement." But having a reserve is crucial for unexpected life events and investment events.

The second reason for the safe reserve is it provides a pool of replacement dollars to purchase new dairy cow stock for the sick or dying dairy cows that inevitably will end up in your investment portfolio.

No matter how well anyone builds a distribution yield focused portfolio, there are going to be dividend cuts, dividend reductions, defaults, bankruptcies, and other events along the way. There's no way to predict the next financial disaster and who that would affect.

Simply accepting that it will happen and at some point you'll need to replace a sick or dead dairy cow investment is the best way to deal with it. I'll give you a few examples to show you just how quickly a dairy cow investment can go from healthy to sick or dead.

Sick or dead cows

Citigroup, Inc. (C) common stock would have been considered a great dairy cow stock up until 2008. From 1986 to the beginning 2008 the company grew its dividend from $0.05 per share to $5.40 per share on a split adjusted basis.[8] Over that same time period, the price per share increased almost 10 fold. It doesn't get much better than that. However, come 2008 and into 2009, your dividend practically disappeared and your share price went from the low $50s down to around $2.

Not only did your income from the stock stop, your principal investment almost disappeared. The cow stopped producing milk and then withered away to nothing, no longer providing much value.

The point of the Citigroup example is not to explain how to avoid holding such a stock, but to illustrate that even the best dairy cow investments can turn into non-income producing penny stocks and that it's important to be prepared for such an occurrence. In the early to mid-2000s, with a $45 share price, a 5%+ yield, and a stable outlook, you'd be a fool not to consider Citigroup common stock a part of your distribution yield focused portfolio.

You'll never be able to avoid every individual stock disaster. The best you can do is diversify your dairy cow investments so no one, two, or three disasters can wipe you out, as well as keep an investable 'safe reserve' to buy more dairy cow investments to replace the income from the ones that died so your retirement income remains the same.

General Electric Co. (GE) is another example of a dairy cow gone bad. While not as big an outright disaster as holding Citigroup (C) stock, stockholders of GE saw a dividend cut as well as significant loss of principal in the panic of 2008 and 2009. This was after a hundred-year history of paying a quarterly dividend.[9] The GE dividend didn't quite disappear – that century-long streak is still intact – but the dividend did shrink from $0.31 per share to $0.10 per share in mid-2009. Around that same time, the share price fell from the high $30 range to below $10 for a time. Distribution yield focused investors saw their income cut by two-thirds and their principal value fall by 75%.

Some of you may be thinking, "Well, of course GE and Citigroup went down with the ship. They got caught up in the sub-prime mortgage mess and had huge financial exposure, which was at the heart of the 2008 to 2009 credit crisis. I saw that coming from a mile away and never would have owned that stock, or I certainly would have sold it before anything bad happened." While hindsight is 20/20, the next market catastrophe will catch just as many investors by surprise and, when looking back, the root of the problems will appear just as obvious.

Again, the point of showing you the examples of GE and Citigroup is not to pretend anyone could ever predict the death or severe sickness of a previously sound dairy cow investment. It's to illustrate the fact that a GE and Citigroup-type outcome will happen to any distribution yield focused investor and that it's crucial to have an investable and safe reserve.

In the case of these two stocks, *the safe reserve gives you liquid dollars to buy income-producing investments to replace the income lost* because of dividend cuts. This would have been easy to do in late 2008 and early 2009. As paralyzing fear gripped the world markets, even investment grade bonds had income yields north of 10% in some cases.

It could have been very easy to allocate less money from your safe reserve than you had even lost in GE and Citigroup to replace the dividend income that those stocks were no longer paying you. The safe reserve allows dairy farmer investors to continue with their retirement lifestyle unchanged despite dairy cow investments "dying" in a portfolio. And by having the safe reserve there all along with the expectation that something like this will eventually happen, it should be an unemotional event to simply allocate these dollars to replace the dividend income lost.

Maturity date controlled fixed income

Now that you understand the need for a safe reserve even within your investable assets, I want to move on to what should be a conservative but income-producing portion of your distribution yield-focused portfolio: a maturity date controlled fixed income allocation. This may be the most novel point that I make in this book because the process of buying individual bonds is fraught with headaches and dangers and the vast majority of investors rely on bond funds to handle their fixed-income exposure.

Few of us are capable of evaluating a company's books to decide if the company is credit worthy or not. And usually if it's obvious that a company is credit worthy, its bonds are over-priced and don't pay enough income to make them worth owning.

Compared to the stock market, looking at the prices paid for individual bonds, the bond market can be inefficient for the small retail investor. Typically, there's a much smaller number of bonds available for purchase and sale. The difference between what the bond is worth and what the investor needs to pay to own the bond can be substantial.

With common stock, usually there are millions of shares floating around and it's very difficult for anyone to charge a markup on these shares of stocks because the buyer can just go elsewhere to buy shares markup free.

With bonds, however, there may be a little more than several thousand of each issue, leaving the would-be buyer without a lot of other choices. This means the dealers holding these bonds can charge a markup.

Institutional investors (like mutual funds) may get better deals when it comes to purchasing bonds as they have more money to buy with (bulk discounts work in investing, too) and can buy directly from the bond issuer, avoiding any mark-up entirely. Because of this, the common advice is to leave the bond investing to the professionals since you'll never be able to duplicate the returns of a well-run bond fund.

If we're looking at total return, that probably is the case. But, as I mentioned before, looking at bonds for total return is the wrong way to go about it. The point is not that you can do it better or outperform professional mutual fund managers, it's just that you have a specific income goal for your bond allocation that the mutual fund managers don't.

In all likelihood, all they care about is generating a total return equal to or greater than the index to which they are benchmarked. It doesn't matter to the mutual fund managers whether or not you need a 4% income yield from your bonds with an average maturity date of 2020 or a 6% income yield with a maturity date of 2025. But *you* care about your specific income as well as when you're getting your money back from the bond issuer, and that makes all of the difference.

Buying individual bonds

The benefits of controlling bond maturity dates as well as aligning your portfolio directly with your income goals outweigh the disadvantages mentioned. By doing some homework, it is possible for the small distribution yield-focused investor to purchase individual bonds successfully.

When I say "homework," I mean investing some of your time into learning how bonds work as well as how they can be bought or sold. If you have no idea where to start, consider subscribing to an investment newsletter that focuses solely on income investments and bonds of all types. This is your retirement we're talking about, so maybe it is worth spending a few hundred dollars for pure third-party bond research that could save you thousands down the road.

You don't need to follow the research and advice in the newsletters to the letter. They'll just give you ideas for where to start and what issues, yields, and maturity dates will make the most sense for your distribution yield-focused portfolio.

As with any income investment, it is important to diversify your bond portfolio between issuers, business sectors, and maturities. Exposure to any individual issue should ideally be less than 1 to 2% of your total investable portfolio.

By keeping exposure to any one bond low as well as laddering bond maturities, your fixed income portfolio should allow you to withstand most interest rate or credit shocks. When I say laddering, I mean spacing maturity dates of the issues you buy so you don't have a large amount of bonds coming due at any one time.

Having some money coming due throughout the duration of your bond portfolio will allow you reduce reinvestment risk – that is, the risk that rates rise and you're stuck with bonds that have dropped in price and are paying below average income.

By making sure you have bonds maturing each year for the next 5 to 10 years (even if you can get higher rates by going out to 15, 20, or 30 years), you can take advantage of a potential increase in rates during that time; with your principal being returned to you, you can then reinvest into the higher income paying bonds that are available. The low-interest rate environment we currently live in makes this an even better idea.

Municipal bonds

Now I want to turn to municipal bonds, which are a bond subset, and highlight another fixed income investment that could add to a distribution yield-focused portfolio: preferred stocks. A municipal bond is debt issued by a local government or entity. Municipal debt can be attractive as it often comes with tax-free interest. For non-retirement account dollars (non-qualified dollars), the ability to earn tax-free interest can be quite attractive.

Not all municipal bonds are federally tax free and some will still be taxable on a state or local level depending on where you reside, but for dairy farmer investors in a higher tax bracket with substantial non-qualified dollars to invest (non-IRA, non-401k, for example), it pays to look at the asset class. You may be saying, "Wait a second. Aren't state and local governments all broke? Why would I want to invest any money in them?"

While many states and local governments are in trouble when it comes to their overall budget, the chance of widespread default is actually quite slim. The overall amount of debt that some local governments own can be a staggering number, but the actual cost to service the debt (pay interest payments to bond holders) can be but a small percentage of the overall municipality's budget.

Also, state and local government officials are unlikely to withhold interest payments from bondholders due to the long-term and dramatic impact default can have on any future borrowing potential.[10] You still may be saying to yourself, "I don't care if municipal governments can afford to pay the interest on the debt per the current budgets. If things get worse, I don't want my retirement income to depend on state or local politicians."

Not all municipal bonds are equal. While being diversified by states and smaller divisions within states, they are also diversified by who pays the bill. Not all municipal bonds depend on the municipal government deciding to include debt payments on the budget. Many municipal bonds are directly linked to a specific development project – an airport or toll road, for example. As long as the project is producing the expected revenue (that is, airlines pay to use gates, people are commuting to work and paying tolls), the interest paid to bondholders shouldn't be in question.

If general obligation bonds (those linked directly to the municipality's ability to budget in debt payments by raising taxes) aren't for you, revenue bonds (those with debt payments linked directly to the revenue from a specific project) may be an alternative.

To understand the potential power of tax-free interest on retirement income, the tax conversion of municipal bond yield is important. Take the yield of a tax-free municipal bond and divide it by the inverse of your tax bracket. You get the taxable equivalent yield that you would need to equal the same amount of income.

For example, if you are in the 25% tax bracket and purchase a municipal bond paying 3.5% tax-free (which certainly doesn't seem like a very high yield), the taxable equivalent yield is:

$$3.5\% / (1-.25) = 3.5\% / .75 = 4.67\%$$

So, you would need to own a taxable bond or other taxable investment paying 4.67% in order to match the income from the lowly 3.5% municipal bond if your interest income would be taxed at 25%. For those in income brackets higher than 25%, the math becomes even more powerful. That same 3.5% municipal bond now pays a tax equivalent 5.79% yield for someone in the 39.6% tax bracket.

$$3.5\% / (1-.396) = 3.5\% / .604 = 5.79\%$$

If you believe tax rates may be increasing for everyone in the future, municipal bonds can be a nice hedge. Historically, the tax-free interest characteristic of municipal bonds has been a non-starter in any debate on what part of the tax code to reform. So, while betting on municipalities may not be a risk-free venture by any means, for dairy farmer investors in higher income tax brackets and with non-qualified dollars to invest, the tax-free interest begs consideration for a portion of a maturity date-controlled fixed income portfolio.

Where do you start when looking to purchase individual municipal bonds so you can control your distribution yield as well as your maturity dates? For the average individual investor, the municipal bond market is even thornier than the taxable bond space. Most investors don't have any idea what a sinking fund is or what the finances of any individual project or county look like.

Relying on the ratings agencies won't help much either. While a good number of municipalities pay to have their bonds rated by various bond-rating agencies, there are plenty of municipalities with great budgets that don't want to incur the added expense to get a rating. So, is a municipal bond trash just because it isn't rated? Not necessarily.

Adding to the confusion are the municipal bond insurers. Does having your municipal bond pay extra to carry insurance against default make sense? On the surface, of course you want the reassurance of knowing that if the municipality stops paying interest to you, someone else will step in to cover the payment.

However, the truth is that the municipal bond insurers have only a fraction of the capital of the overall municipal bond market and would be quickly overwhelmed if there were a large number of defaults. It pays to spend some money on good research or hire a municipal bond broker to help you build a portfolio.

Preferred stock

Despite their name, preferred stocks act like a bond/stock hybrid by providing a high regular income payment as well as offering a fixed value at which they can be redeemed (typically $25 per share). There are too many characteristics of preferred stock to cover here, but a general characteristic of preferred stocks is that they offer more safety than common stock.

Preferred dividends need to be paid before common stock dividends get declared. So, the income stream may be a little safer. Also, preferred shareholder rights are above those of common stock holders in the event of a company bankruptcy but below those of bond holders – hence the "hybrid" characteristic pointed out above.

Preferred stocks can be a safer and higher income way to gain exposure to a certain company. As most preferred stocks seem to be issued from financial services companies, this point can be particularly appropriate today.

An investor may not want to hold Goldman Sachs, Bank of America, Citigroup, or Morgan Stanley common stock because of the real or perceived risk still present in the global financial system. Plus, the dividends paid on those common stocks aren't that appealing from an income-oriented investor's point of view.

If you begin to look at the preferred stocks of those four companies, the risk/reward conversation changes. Instead of betting on growth and the increase or reinstatement of a dividend among the leading financial companies, you simply need the company to continue to pay the 6% yield on its preferred stock, essentially by staying in business.

In some cases, the price of these preferred stocks is still below the $25 par value at which the preferred stocks can be called back by the issuer – meaning the investor could stand to see principal growth as well as income should the market begin to price financial institution investments more favorably.

The downsides to preferred stocks, other than the risk of issuer default, are interest rate risk, similar to any fixed income investment, and a long or perpetual maturity.

While shorter-dated preferred stocks exist, more often than not, the maturity date is decades into the future or perpetual. The issuer can always call the shares back but there isn't a set maturity date. So, with such long maturities in most cases, exposure of your maturity date controlled fixed income portfolio should be limited.

To counter interest rate risk, there are preferred stocks that have a floating-rate coupon – a distribution that is tied to some measure of interest rates that will rise or fall with that index. If buying such a long-dated fixed income security with a fixed coupon scares you because of the risk of rising interest rates, preferred stocks can still be a valuable holding if you turn to the floating rate issues.

Whether you allocate a large or small percentage of your investable portfolio to fixed income, you need to control and ladder maturity dates of the individual investments, and diversify among the multiple classes of fixed income available. Should interest rates rise, you'll be better able to preserve principal as well as take advantage of the rising rates by reinvesting your fixed income dollars at higher rates as your holdings mature over time.

CHAPTER 6

Dividend Superstars

For purchasing power protection, the dairy cows that are "dividend superstars" need to be the core of any retiree's income portfolio. An investable reserve is critical and a maturity controlled bond portfolio is nice to have for more stability and a firm date on the return of your principal. But nothing will do the heavy lifting to provide a growing stream of income like solid dividend paying common stocks.

It's not only about the income that is produced from your portfolio during the first year of retirement. You need to ensure your portfolio income distribution yield keeps up with the inflation of your living expenses. You don't want to liquidate principal a few years down the road because your living expenses increase.

Not every dividend payer is super

How do you select your dairy cows? Do you simply search for the highest yielding dividend paying stocks and buy those? It's not that simple.

Just because a dairy cow is producing lots of milk right now (a dividend stock paying a huge current dividend) doesn't mean that dairy cow will keep producing the same amount of milk forever. Sometimes a high current yield can be a sign of danger and certainly warrants a closer look. While it's important to make sure the dividend income of your dairy cow stocks is high enough to meet your current distribution yield goals, it's more important to ensure that the income streams are safe and show a history of regularly increasing.

I used 3M Co. (MMM) as an example earlier in the book to show the difference between price and dividend income. In this case, the dividend increased each year despite a very difficult economic environment.

So, how do you go about looking for healthy dairy cows that pay a solid current yield and also show promise of increasing the dividend each year?

Identifying companies that pay a dividend is a good first step. Rather than buying a fast growing company that doesn't pay a dividend and hoping that will change, it's better to go with a stock that has an established track record of returning money to shareholders.

Any current dividend yield north of 2%-2.5% would be a good floor. From there, you want to assess the safety of that dividend before moving forward. A good ratio check is the dividend payout ratio: the amount of a company's earnings being returned to shareholders in the form of dividend payments.

Almost any financial website will display the current dividend payment in the form of a dollar amount per share as well as the company's current Earnings Per Share, or EPS. It is important to verify the exact frequency of the dividend since it will influence the calculation of the dividend payout ratio. Most dividends are paid quarterly, so you'll need to take the per-share dividend listed and multiply that amount by 4 to come up with an annualized amount that matches the EPS number, which represents a full year.

Johnson & Johnson's (JNJ) numbers in early 2012 provide a good example. At that time, the stock paid a dividend of $0.57 per share, which equaled roughly a 3.5% yield (total dividends divided by the share price). The earnings per share of JNJ was $5 even. By taking the dividend amount, multiplying by 4, and then dividing that number by the EPS, you get your dividend payout ratio.

$$\$0.57 \times 4 = \$2.28 \,/\, \$5 = 45.6\%$$

What that tells us is that Johnson & Johnson is paying out 45.6% of its earnings in the form of dividends to shareholders. By itself, that doesn't mean much. It can signify, though, that earnings per share would need to take a significant hit before any negative change to the dividend per share amount might take place. It's telling you that Johnson & Johnson has put in place a significant cushion to protect the per share dividend amount and even if earnings remain stagnant, there is probably room to increase the dividend.

Could Johnson & Johnson raise the payout ratio to 60% and thus increase current shareholder's income? Certainly, but the dairy cow investment is choosing a safer path by maintaining a cushion of safety in the payout ratio.

It's hard to pinpoint the exact ratio that should represent a warning sign to income investors. Each company is different and derives its earnings in different ways. Typically, a ratio less than 65% to 75% could be viewed as allowing a cushion unless you're evaluating a Real Estate Investment Trust (REIT), Business Development Company (BDC), Master Limited Partnership (MLP), or other income-oriented investment.

It's important to note that EPS can be impacted drastically in the short-term by one-time expenses, as corporate accounting can be quite complicated. However, it's better to deal with the exceptions to the payout ratio rule than try to incorporate every what-if scenario. In general, by examining the payout ratio, the distribution yield-focused investor can get a good idea of the health of the selected dairy cow investments.

Dividend history and dividend growth

After looking for a high enough but safely covered dividend, the next step in selecting dairy cow dividend paying stocks would be to review the dividend history to determine the pattern of regular and predictable growth of the dividend. Most financial websites provide this information if you look for the "dividend history." The company's investor relations website can also be very useful in finding the pattern of dividend increases or decreases.

Abbott Laboratories (ABT) is the next example. In late 2011-early 2012, ABT paid $0.48 per share in quarterly dividends easily covered by the $3.01 earnings per share and resulting in roughly a 3.5%

current yield. Looking deeper into the company's history shows that the first dividend of 2012 was the 352nd quarterly dividend paid by the company and that dividend payments had increased for 39 consecutive years.[11] So, is it safe to say that ABT satisfies the first three qualifications?

Good current yield, check. Good dividend payout ratio, check. Consistent history of shareholder-friendly dividend policies, check. The common stocks remaining after these three qualifiers should be a good starting list for choosing your dairy cow investments.

Diversify

It's important to consider diversification across industry, size, and geography. You'll notice that Johnson & Johnson (JNJ) and Abbott Laboratories (ABT) are both classified as healthcare stocks. Simply loading up on them because they fit the first three characteristics of a "dividend superstar" isn't prudent. The portfolio lacks diversification across different business sectors.

Diversification by industry or sector is easy to evaluate. You'll want your dairy cow dividend stocks to represent everything from healthcare to finance to consumer goods to real estate and anything in between. That way, a downturn in any one part of the economy won't drastically affect the income produced by your distribution yield-focused portfolio.

Diversify by size

Size can be evaluated by looking at the market capitalization of each stock and ensuring you have some smaller-sized dividend payers mixed in with the giants like Procter & Gamble (PG) and Johnson & Johnson (JNJ) to help diversify your dividend income stream.

Just because a company is small doesn't mean it isn't just as safe as a larger one or can't pay a meaningful and increasing dividend. Remember, the giant large cap stocks of the world all started as small companies at some point.

So, what is market capitalization and what does it mean for you? It is the number of outstanding shares multiplied by the share price. For example, a company with 1 million shares outstanding and a $40 share price would have a market capitalization of $40 million. On its own, the calculation doesn't do much for you. But when you compare it to the market capitalization of thousands of other companies that have their stocks listed, you'll get an idea of where your company falls on the size scale.

Typically, the standards for size dictate that a "large cap" company has a market capitalization of more than $10 billion, a "mid cap" company has a market capitalization of between $2 billion and $10 billion, and a "small cap" company has a market capitalization of under $2 billion. Most of the "brand name" stocks that you hear about every day in the marketplace will be large cap stocks.

It is easy to just focus on investing in the names you recognize, especially when it comes to dividend payers (larger companies with more predictable earnings and cash flow). However, a properly diversified dairy cow portfolio requires the inclusion of the smaller and under-the-radar dairy cow investments. Don't worry. There are plenty out there to choose from.

To illustrate the point that bigger isn't necessarily better and that quality dividend-paying small cap stocks do exist is Healthcare Services Group (HCSG). . You probably haven't heard of the company but can guess at what it does from the company name. This provider of laundry, housekeeping, and dining services to custodial care facilities isn't a new company. Healthcare Services Group went public in 1983. Also, the company has increased its dividend every quarter for almost the last 10 years.[12]

Healthcare Services Group fits the three dividend superstar criteria we established; it just happens to be a smaller company posting a market cap of around $1.6 billion. Just because you haven't heard of the company doesn't mean it's not worthy of inclusion in your dividend stock portfolio. If anything, it's that much more important to include companies like Healthcare Services Group to provide size diversification and hopefully smooth out some of the inevitable market ups and downs. If all large cap stocks perform poorly for whatever reason, it's nice to own smaller names that produce just as much income but potentially provide better growth opportunities.

Diversify globally

In addition to diversifying by business and size, with the ever-increasing globalization of the world economy and markets, diversifying by geography will become more and more important. So you're saying, "Great. Not only do I have to find small dividend paying companies I've never heard of, but now I'm going to have to invest in a company that's halfway around the world and that I know nothing about." Actually, no.

Plenty of good dividend-paying companies are worth taking a look at in Europe, South America, Australia, and Japan. But, a dairy cow investor hoping to diversify dividend income streams by geography doesn't need to look any further than a company like Procter & Gamble Co. (PG). You may be saying, "Procter & Gamble? They're based in Cincinnati! How is that company anything close to international?"

What's more important than the physical location of the company is the physical location of sales – that is, where a company with a global reach derives its revenue. Many "domestic" companies are anything but when you look deeper into the revenue numbers. For example, Procter & Gamble Co. gets more than half of its revenue from overseas sources.[13]

Also, Procter & Gamble isn't unique in this respect. Plenty of companies that are considered "All-American" have a huge presence overseas, including Wal-Mart, Johnson & Johnson, and Ford. The point is to not look solely at where companies are headquartered to assess an income portfolio's level of geographical diversification. In order to gather whether the stock you own gives you international exposure, digging a little deeper into the revenue sources helps tremendously.

Having investment and particularly dividend-paying stock exposure outside of the United States isn't an academic exercise. Since you have to rely on your dairy cow investments to not only maintain their dividends but hopefully grow them, you want the underlying companies to have some type of growth strategy.

A mature, multinational dividend payer has two avenues of growth: more sales from existing customers, or new customers. Looking at the United States, while there may always be room for growth via existing consumers, there comes a point when the market share for a particular product becomes too saturated and costly to grow. However, tremendous growth opportunities exist outside of the United States where an emerging consumer has never had access or the ability to purchase the very goods we take for granted.

Any dividend superstar worth an investment better be positioned to gain new customers in the emerging economies across the world. That emerging economies around the world represent huge sources of potential customer growth isn't a secret and almost every multinational dividend payer is clamoring for a piece of the pie. Fortunately, the pie has just started growing in many places and for the time being, innovative first-entrants as well as followers should all benefit.

It is less important to choose the ultimate "winner" in the fight for market share among emerging market consumers than it is to ensure your dairy cow investments are at least part of the international growth equation.

Limit position size

Finally, the simplest but most effective way to diversify your dividend superstar portfolio is to limit position size. If there's one thing investors can count on, it's the certainty of uncertainty. As I mentioned before, seemingly indestructible business models can be reduced to nothing rather quickly and exceptional dairy cow investments can become exceptionally bad.

Rather than risk the futility of guessing how and when disaster will eventually befall a once dividend superstar, limit each dividend-paying stock to less than 1 to 2% of your overall investable portfolio. This size limit will help preserve principal as well as distribution yield should a few dividend-paying stocks go bankrupt or simply reduce or suspend a dividend.

It's rare that a healthy dividend-paying company would suddenly find itself in severe financial distress. More likely, a dividend payer would need to reduce the per share payout due to lower-than-expected earnings.

By limiting any one stock to less than 1 to 2% of your distribution yield portfolio, you should be able to manage the event as well as not have to take a huge portion of your safe reserve to purchase a replacement if necessary

---

How to select dividend superstars

- Look for a good current yield; use a dividend yield floor of 2% to 2.5%.
- Watch the payout ratio.
- Look for a history of dividends being paid as well as annual or quarterly growth of the dividend.
- Diversify across multiple business sectors.
- Diversify by size.
- Diversify globally.
- Limit investment in any one company to less than 1 to 2% of your overall portfolio.
- Be wary of high-yielding stocks (dividend yields north of 5% to 6%); they are not necessarily bad investments but be cautious and do your research.

CHAPTER 7

Alternative Income Producers

The first three parts of a distribution yield-focused portfolio having been constructed, an income investor may find that the income produced from the maturity date controlled bond portfolio and the dividend paying stocks (combined with a non-income producing safe reserve) isn't enough to reach the desired income goal. This is not the time to start choosing riskier bonds or only very high yielding dividend paying stocks. The next two parts of a distribution yield focused portfolio allow a dairy farmer investor to increase income while also increasing diversification without compromising the basic dairy farmer investment principles.

The fourth portfolio allocation, which I've called "Alternative Income Producers," provides diversification for the distribution yield-focused portfolio through access to non-traditional income producing assets, adding other income producing investments such as Real Estate Investment Trusts (REITs), Business Development Companies (BDCs), and Master Limited Partnerships (MLPs) to the more common and widely held stocks and bonds I discussed earlier in the book.

Because REITs, BDCs, and MLPs typically yield more than most traditional dividend paying stocks or investment grade bonds, the income-focused investor can further diversify the retirement income stream by hedging against one asset class performing badly and still increase the overall distribution yield of the portfolio.

Do these higher-yielding investments mean they are riskier asset classes? Not necessarily. To explain why, let me first go into the basics of each.

REITs

A Real Estate Investment Trust is a business entity (typically a partnership) specifically structured to avoid tax at the corporate or trust level. The tax code allows a REIT to largely avoid taxation as long as it distributes 90% of its earnings to shareholders (or unit holders as is often the case with partnership status). You may remember that the magic dividend payout ratio we established earlier was no higher than 75%. Now we have an investment that is actually bound by the tax code to pay out 90% of earnings. How can that be safe?

REITs can be a great asset class to own due to the nature of the business, and distribution yield-focused investors still have plenty of opportunity to find a stable and growing stream of income in the real estate asset class. As investors in real estate, REITs don't need to worry about growth through innovation or growing product sales to an expanding consumer base. They buy a piece of real estate and lease out the property to generate income for the partners and unit holders. Hopefully, this is a very straightforward, even boring, business model: maintain real estate properties to keep them attractive, ensure lessees pay their rents, and distribute at least 90% of this very predictable rental income to the shareholders.

Short-term history shows us that the business can be anything but boring, however. Beginning with the sub-prime mortgage crisis in 2007 and carrying through the recession of 2008 and 2009, everything from residential to commercial to hotels to industrial properties experienced huge upheaval as individuals as well as businesses stopped paying their mortgages or rents. A drive through any urban or suburban landscape around this time would have shown you the effects of this event, with empty storefronts and for sale signs more numerous to count.

But like any investment, not all REITs are created equal. They come in all different shapes and sizes with some specializing in residential real estate while others focus on retail; some only buy hotels while others concentrate on senior living facilities. Some

REITs will even avoid owning any property outright and just supply the financing (a mortgage REIT).

The last few years of upheaval have affected the various kinds of REITs very differently. While many REITs got in trouble between 2007 and 2009, just as many cruised through the general downturn in real estate with their real estate portfolios and income distributions intact.

I will give an example to help prove the point that REITs should be an almost essential part of a portfolio for the investor looking for stable and growing income.

Below is a chart for the aptly named Realty Income Corp. (O) showing five years of stock price history as well as five years of dividend payout history from early 2007 to early 2012.

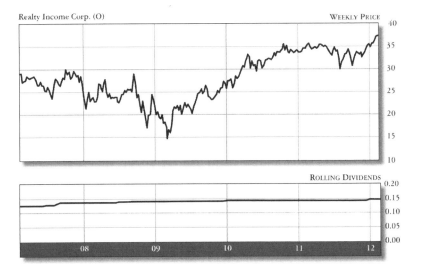

Notice the price volatility over the five-year time period; also notice the dividend, which wasn't just stable but increased through one of the roughest real estate markets in decades. Long-time holders of O wouldn't have been surprised by the performance.

Realty Income Corp. calls itself "The Monthly Dividend Company®" and has a 42-year track record of maintaining a monthly dividend.[14] Not all REITs pay monthly income – in fact, most don't.

O decided to make this its policy. Realty Income Corp. has also increased the dividend 63 times over those same 42 years.

What allowed the company to emerge from the downturn with a higher dividend? Like anything in real estate, the answer is location, location, location. Also, it doesn't hurt that Realty Income Corp. diversifies over hundreds of tenants, geography, and employs triple-net leases in most cases.

Realty Income Corp. owns mostly freestanding single-tenant buildings in prime locations, which helps immensely during economic downturns, when prized locations tend to fare better than others. Also, having multiple tenants and holding properties across the United States rather than in just one region makes sense; it reduces the impact a downturn may have on your rental income in any one industry or location.

Triple-net leases are a huge part of the equation as well. A triple-net lease basically means that although the REIT owns the physical property, the tenant pays maintenance, taxes, and insurance costs. The REIT just collects the rent checks and distributes the income to the unit holders – not a bad deal. Looking at Realty Income Corp., it's easy to see why the distribution yield-focused investor holding the REIT from 2007 to 2009 fared just fine.

Before investing in any REIT though, make sure you've taken a look at the properties the REIT holds as well as the lease structure. This will give you good insight into whether the REIT is diversified, can handle adverse economic conditions, and can match rental rates to inflation.

Non-traded REITs

O is a good example of a REIT that trades on an exchange just like stock. This allows an investor to buy or sell it at any time just like any other dividend paying stock. Liquidity is nice but the income focused investor also needs to deal with the ups and downs of the market. As you can see from the five-year chart of O, even though the dividend remained stable, the stock price declined almost 50% at one point.

I've explained why the dairy farmer investor should not be concerned with stock price movements of a healthy dairy cow investment. However, within the REIT space, there is an alternative to the roller coaster ride.

A non-traded REIT is an investment portfolio of properties that does not trade on any exchange. If it doesn't trade on an exchange, how does an investor purchase shares? Typically, an investor can purchase shares of a non-traded REIT through a broker and a subscription agreement with the entity that manages the REIT.

In most cases, a non-traded REIT is a start-up portfolio that owns no property initially. By gathering investor deposits, it will purchase properties as dictated by its prospectus. This offering period can last for years in some cases. When a targeted dollar amount is reached, the non-traded REIT will close to new investors and then simply manage the portfolio for income and/or growth for the benefit of the existing unit holders.

Eventually, the managing entity will try to create a liquidity event for the shareholders; this could include an outright sale of the portfolio or a listing of the non-traded REIT on an exchange, which would then make it a traded REIT. In fact, some traded REITs today started out through this exact process.

The general idea of a non-traded REIT allows investors to gain access to an investment portfolio built from scratch without any overhang from "legacy" investments that could be both good or bad. The managing entity will attempt to provide additional value by building a portfolio that can then be sold or listed for a higher share price than the original investors paid. There are several risks to the non-traded REIT approach.

Risks of non-traded REITs

First, the managing entity may purchase poor assets or overpay for properties. This can occur because as money flows in from the initial investors, the non-traded REIT may feel pressured to put these funds to work regardless of the market conditions. Investors probably don't want to see their REIT sitting largely in un-invested cash, even if it might be the best thing at the moment.

Second, a few layers of fees exist before the initial investors will see any profit. The fees paid to the brokers can sometimes be in the 5 to 10% range.

Third, a non-traded REIT is an extremely illiquid investment. If the portfolio isn't being run to the investor's liking or performance has been poor, there's not a whole lot that investor can do. Some non-traded REITs do allow investors to sell the shares back to the managing entity after a few years have passed (typically four), without incurring additional surrender fees. However, surrender fees may exist on other non-traded REITsntil a liquidity event occurs.

Fourth, even though a non-traded REIT can't be bought or sold on an exchange (or redeemed without a penalty), once it closes the offering to new investors, it must report a price (required by Financial Industry Regulatory Authority, or FINRA) at least every 18 months. So, if real estate market conditions are bad, it is possible for a non-traded REIT investor to see a loss of principal despite the potential lack of a market for the investment.

Advantages of non-traded REITs

What could the benefits of non-traded REITs possibly be over traded REITs? One potential psychological advantage is the fact that re-pricing can be limited to 18 months. In severe market dislocations, a traded REIT could drop 50% like we saw in 2008 and 2009. While the non-traded REIT might eventually re-price lower as well, maintaining a static principal value will at least provide a temporary bright spot.

Again, I hope I have convinced you to divorce market price from income, so this benefit should really be a moot point for the dairy farmer investor. However, the one benefit of some non-traded REITs that's hard to argue against is the compounding boost provided by reinvestment of dividends at a discount.

Some non-traded REITs will reward unit holders who automatically reinvest dividends to have these dividends purchase shares at a 5% discount. As a new portfolio, the REIT benefits by having more dollars to invest, so it makes sense to them to allow the discount to then have the reinvested dividends to work with as well.

This discounted reinvestment price is powerful for the investor who can wait 5-10 years before wanting income distributions. By purchasing a non-traded REIT and taking advantage of the automatic dividend reinvestment at a 5% discount, the eventual income yield when the distributions are needed could be substantially higher than if no discount was given. The investor can stop reinvesting the dividends at any time and receive the now "bonus"-compounded income like any other investment.

It used to be more common for individual stocks to offer dividend reinvestment discounts if the shares were held directly with the company (or appointed transfer agent) but this is rare today. This added compounding boost means non-traded REITs could be an attractive alternative for the dairy cow investor during the income distribution phase.

BDCs

Business Development Companies (BDCs) are similar to REITs. They are required to pay out 90% of taxable income in the form of dividends to avoid taxation at the entity level. Changes in tax law in 1980 brought BDCs into existence, serving as lenders to smaller, private companies that may not have access to the capital markets like a larger traded company. Compared to REITs, I would characterize BDCs as one more step up the risk ladder. Investors typically get compensated for the additional risk.

Yields on BDCs often exceed 10%.The high yield is possible because of what BDCs do. Being one of the only ways for small or private companies to raise cash, BDCs can command much higher interest rates and better terms than a typical bond offering, equity issuance, or banking loan.

Often, BDCs secure these high interest rate loans to equipment or other tangible assets in the case of default. Also, BDCs may get a piece of equity ownership from the small and/or private company on top of the loan interest they are already getting paid.

In general, a BDC will succeed if the companies they loan to are profitable. With such good terms comes the risk that the borrower's growth plans don't pan out. As a result, I place such high-yield lending practices in a higher-risk basket compared to other stocks, bonds, or alternative investments.

Prospect Capital Corp. (PSEC) is a good example of the high-yield/high-risk nature of BDCs. The following five-year chart is constructed similarly to other charts I have shown you, but the bottom box shows the current yield of PSEC over the five-year time frame rather than the rolling dividend.

A few years ago PSEC changed the frequency at which it paid its dividend (going to a monthly payout), so comparisons on a dollar amount per share won't be useful. While yield will be more volatile, it demonstrates a potentially high distribution yield if the dairy cow investor can stomach the ride.

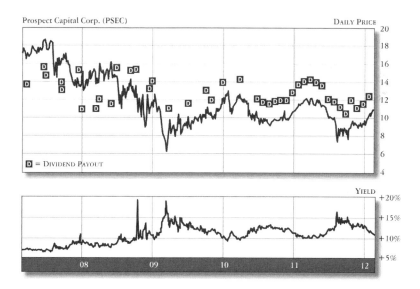

While the stock price has been all over the place, with the current yield moving correspondingly (remember, yield is a function of the dividend amount divided by the current share price), the distribution yield has generally been above 10%. PSEC did reduce its dividend by 25% in early 2010 by shifting from a roughly $0.40 per quarter dividend to a roughly $0.10 per month dividend.

Because the stock price fell during that same period, the current yield stayed about the same. Remember, though, the shareholder at that time would have seen a 25% dividend reduction as well as roughly a 20% principal decline.

Tips for investing in BDCs

I have developed a set of tips that should be helpful to you when investing in BDCs. First, a BDC's performance can tend to match the general economy. While there will always be exceptions in any economic environment, it typically is easier for small companies to thrive if the economy as a whole is doing well. The 2008-2010 period was not a thriving economic time. But, if you believe that the economy may improve moving forward, BDCs may be a good high-yielding way to play that growth as their loan portfolios should perform better if the borrowers are around and growing.

Second, try to purchase BDCs when they trade close to their book value. Book value is essentially the net worth of a company; assets minus liabilities. It is the amount a company should technically be worth if it were to be liquidated.

Many financial websites will publish a figure called "price to book," or Price/Book. If this ratio is one, you know the price of the outstanding shares is roughly worth the value of a company. With BDCs, delivering a high-yielding investment at a reasonable valuation can provide a rewarding yield for the risk.

With all high yielding investments comes risk, but BDCs can be a great way to purchase a liquid, exchange-traded investment that can pay a distribution yield north of 10%. Even allocating a small percentage of your overall portfolio to BDCs can raise the overall distribution yield and produce a more comfortable retirement income without having to liquidate principal.

MLPs

I want to walk you through the final acronym presented as part of the "Alternative Income Producers" section: Master Limited Partnerships (MLPs). An MLP gets the same preferential tax treatment of avoiding taxes at the entity level. It is typically engaged in the production or transportation of oil and/or natural gas. Most MLPs essentially serve as the toll road operators for the energy industry.

Once natural gas or oil is pumped out of the ground, it needs to make its way from the drill site to the end user. MLPs construct, own, and operate the pipelines through which the oil or gas flows. What makes this business model unique and potentially very profitable are the high barriers to entry.

When a pipeline is approved, has cleared the environmental hurdles, and has been constructed, it is very unlikely a competing pipeline will be approved to serve the same area. That initial pipeline becomes a "toll road" type of business.

While MLPs do have some exposure to the raw price of the physical commodity through production or storage operations, as long as oil or gas flows through the pipelines from point A to point B, it doesn't matter if gas or oil prices are high or low; MLPs will collect their toll.

Looking at the next few decades of U.S. energy production, MLPs should continue to be profitable as the shale deposits just being tapped now will supply both domestic and growing international energy demand.

MLPs with prime pipeline locations (from shale deposits to large urban areas or port cities for export overseas) can provide a dairy farmer investor with a potentially stable and growing income stream for years to come.

MLPs do have a few disadvantages for investors. First, MLPs issue K-1 tax forms to unit holders each year. The K-1s break down the portion of the investor's dividend income that is taxable and the portion that is considered a pass-through loss. While this tax deferral can be helpful, K-1s typically don't get issued until March – sometimes later in the month. An investor who is used to completing a tax return in February, when most other tax forms are issued, will see MLPs upset this process.

Second, to avoid any Unrelated Business Taxable Income (UBTI) issues, you should discuss ownership of MLPs in a qualified account with a tax professional. Because of the K-1 pass through of losses and declaration of ordinary income, UBTI can be triggered in IRA accounts and cause the investment to become taxable when it would normally be tax deferred as it is held in an IRA.

I won't pick out a particular example of an MLP right now. Almost any MLP investment has performed very well over the past decade. In addition to growing distributions, investors in MLPs over the past years have sometimes seen considerable price appreciation as well. The dairy farmer investor looking at MLPs for the first time should focus on those with the best positioned operations and opportunities to increase the income distribution for unit holders.

Alternative investments and the dairy farmer investor

These three alternative high-income investments should help increase a dairy farmer investor's distribution yield. They also add diversification and the potential for purchasing power protection through growing income streams. REITs, BDCs, and MLPs, which are outside the realm of the typical bonds and stocks, allow a distribution yield-focused investor to target an overall portfolio income yield north of 5% without having to take on inordinate risk.

Investment alternatives like these, especially in a low interest rate environment, are extremely powerful. As a rule, though, I would limit your overall "Alternative Income Producers" allocation to 25% or less of your overall five-part portfolio. That should allow enough exposure to have a positive impact on the overall portfolio yield without concentrating too many dollars in any one type of investment.

CHAPTER 8

High Income
(But Not Necessarily High Risk)

The fifth part of the distribution yield-focused portfolio, High Income, can now be put in place with any remaining dollars. If you've managed to meet your income goal through the first four parts described already, then great, you may not need to worry about creating additional income opportunities.

If you're a distribution yield-focused investor interested in creating double-digit percentage yields on stocks that you may already own, you'll want to pay close attention to the strategies outlined in this chapter. Even if it means you'll have just extra dollars to spend on vacations or as gifts for family members, implementing a "High Income But Not High Risk" portion of your portfolio can be a worthwhile undertaking.

Options

Options came into existence in financial markets in 1973, when the Chicago Board Options Exchange (CBOE) created a standardized and enforceable contract and clearing mechanism for traders.[15] While options can be used to place bets on rising or falling prices of a particular stock or good, they can also be used to reduce or hedge risks or exposures.

If I've already lost you with the word "options," please bear with me. I'll be looking at using options for the income-oriented investor only via covered calls. With covered calls, investors pay no money up front and the biggest risks are that, after the covered call option expires, you're still holding the same stock as before or you just made a profit.

With a covered call, you're selling someone the right to purchase the stock you already own at a pre-set price with a pre-set expiration date. That's it. By giving someone this right, they will pay you immediately and in full the presumed value of this right. So from day one, you will have collected cash, which can't be taken away regardless of whether the option is assigned or expires worthless.

Typically, the value of the call option "premium" can be a few percent of the overall stock position, but can be as much as 10%, depending on the option's time frame. Covered calls are a great way to take a low or non-income paying stock position and turn it into a high yield position without increasing the risk of owning the stock. I'll start with a few examples of covered calls on stocks you would probably own anyway as a dairy farmer investor.

Covered calls on a dividend superstar

According to our previously established qualifiers, Intel Corp. (INTC) would be a dividend superstar dairy cow investment that a distribution yield-focused investor would want to own anyway. You have a multinational company with the ability to increase cash flow as well as produce an increasing dividend. But what if it were possible to turn the 3% annual income yield on INTC into a 10% to 15% annual yield without taking on additional risk? That's exactly what a covered call strategy can do.

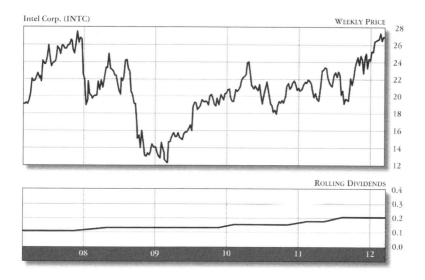

Intel Corp. (INTC) — Weekly Price / Rolling Dividends

As you can see from the five-year stock price and rolling dividend chart, investors that bought shares in February 2012 in this scenario would pay around $27 per share. By giving the right to someone else to buy shares of INTC at $28 in July 2012, investors would earn a 4% return. That doesn't include the price appreciation of $1 that investors would also earn should INTC reach $28 by July. That 4% also doesn't include the dividends that would be collected during the next five months either. Here's how the numbers work.

On February 26, 2012, INTC was trading for around $27.28. The call option with a strike price of $28 on INTC for July 2012 carried a premium of $1.13 per share. This covered call strategy can work for someone just looking to buy INTC for the first time or for someone who has held the shares for years. In either case, once the INTC shares are owned, investors would simply sell the July calls and earn $1.13 per share for their trouble.

The $1.13 divided into the current share price of $27.28 comes out to 4.15% – not a bad immediate return for a day's work. From now until the third Friday in July, the covered call strategy is quite boring.

While Intel stock as well as the call options will move up or down in price over the next 5 months, not much else will happen.

Technically, the option can be exercised and call away the INTC shares at any time, but this is a rare occurrence.

Investors will collect dividends as they still own the stock outright, so the dividend record date in May will trigger the dividend to be delivered to investors sometime in early June.[16] On the 3rd Friday in July, it essentially comes down to whether or not INTC is trading above or below $28 per share.

If INTC was above $28, it will most likely be called away and investors would be given $28 in cash for each share owned regardless of where INTC is actually trading.

If INTC is below $28, the call option will likely expire worthless and the investor will still own the same shares and can repeat the same process. I say likely, as options can be exercised even if the stock price is slightly below the strike price. Its not all that likely, but it is a possibility.

Even if the call option is exercised and the cash delivered at $28 per share, the investor can turn right around and buy shares of INTC again and do the same thing over. So where do the return numbers get us?

For those five months, we already know the investor earned 4.15% just for selling the call option. Also, the investor would have earned a .75% dividend with the one quarterly dividend payment occurring during that time. Then, add in the $0.72 of price appreciation from where INTC was at when the calls were sold ($27.28 versus the $28 option target price) – another 2.63% ($0.72 dividend by $27.28).

Without including the price appreciation component (if INTC never gets called away), the income produced by this strategy each year will be between 9% and 11% if investor only get to sell two rounds of covered calls because five-month periods don't exactly fit nicely into 12-month calendar years. If the calendar worked out so that three option periods could be used, 15% total income was possible from the call premiums received as well as the yearly dividend yield of 3%.

Negating risks

Income potential like this on a stock you would want to own anyway may sound too good to be true, but it isn't. A covered call strategy just like the one I've outlined can be done with many other solid, dividend paying dairy cow investments. However, I do want to highlight the risks involved with a covered call strategy and how to negate many of them.

The two biggest risks involved are severe movements down, as well as up, in the underlying stock's price. Since investors have given up the right to the shares until a point several months into the future, they must hold those shares until that time no matter what the movements are in the underlying stock. (There are ways to close out covered call positions prior to option expiration but I won't go into them here.)

If the share price falls, investors get to keep the call premium, but have depreciated shares for future investment. If the share price soars, investors' gains are capped as they would be required to sell the shares to the call option holder at the specified price even if the market price of the shares were much higher. These two risks can be negated by proper security selection.

When I say proper security selection, covered calls should be used only with stocks that you would want to own anyway. INTC was a great example. As a dairy cow investment, you would want to own the stock if it were $28 per share or $15 per share. As long as the dividend was intact, it wouldn't matter. The same work that would go into owning any dividend paying stock should apply to a stock owned for covered calls.

One of the biggest obstacles to a covered call strategy is greed. Investors need to understand that the dividend plus the call premium is the only return expected. Should the underlying stock soar in price and the gains are capped by the call option execution price, investors have a serious problem if they are upset by 8 to 10% gains.

You can't look back and say, "If I had only held the stock outright and not sold the calls, I would have ridden the stock all the way up." It's important to remember why you are doing the covered call strategy in the first place: It's an income yield in the neighborhood of 10% plus.

When a stock doesn't make the dividend superstar shortlist

The next covered call example involves a stock that you may want to own but that doesn't carry a high enough dividend yield to be included in the "dividend superstar" allocation. By using a stock like this in a covered call strategy, you'll get to own the stock you like and still generate an income stream to help boost your overall portfolio's distribution yield.

Owners of energy assets very rarely do their own drilling or extraction. Instead, the Exxons, Chevrons, and BPs of the world hire an expert to do this highly specialized work for them. Schlumberger Ltd. (SLB) is one of the leading energy service companies.

With the search for more oil and gas only growing, Schlumberger stands to benefit from its well-positioned role as extraction specialist. Oil and gas companies looking to develop a particular asset choose the driller with the most expertise, experience, and innovative technology. This provides a nice advantage and business moat for a company like Schlumberger.

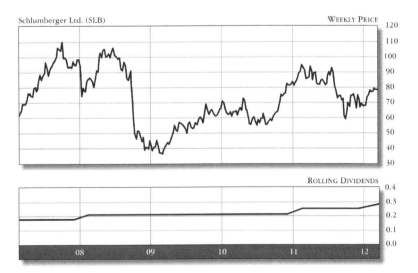

While the global exposure to the energy industry as well as the business model may make you want to own SLB shares, the company lacks a high current dividend yield (only around 1.4%) or an established dividend history. Therefore, SLB may not make the short list of dairy cow investments. However, by writing covered call options, investors can gain exposure to the stock as well as serve their overall income goal, getting the best of both worlds.

Let's look at the actual numbers. Purchasing shares of SLB in late February 2012 would have cost around $78 per share. At that time, the August 2012 (approximately six months into the future) $80 call had a price of around $5.55 per share. Dividing $5.55 into $78, we learn that the investor using this covered call strategy would make 7.1% immediately by purchasing SLB shares and then selling the August $80 calls – not a bad income yield for the next six months.

Annualizing this yield (assuming the investor can sell calls again once the August calls expire) brings the yield to around 14%. That doesn't include any dividends paid by SLB, nor does it assume the $2 of capital appreciation per share should SLB get called away in August.

Here, covered calls allow an investor to own an otherwise low-income stock and still produce a very high-income yield that can increase the overall distribution yield of the retirement portfolio.

Highlighting the risks of this scenario, investor need to realize that they'll have to hold onto SLB shares from now until the option expiration even if SLB soars or plummets in price. Buying a stock you would want to own anyway (a leader in the energy service sector) and entering into the covered call with the right mindset (accepting 7.1% as your six-month return), these two risks can be understood and accepted.

Come August, investors will always be able to write more calls should the price of SLB fall, or have the proceeds of $80 per share in cash (assuming SLB shares appreciated and got called away at the option strike price) to reinvest. These are not horrible outcomes as long as the risks are understood.

The scenario with SLB demonstrates that not every investment you own needs to be producing high levels of dividend income. In some cases, you may have legacy assets from inheritances or slow accumulation over time that you simply don't want to sell outright to reinvest in income producers.

With a covered call strategy, you can generate income on these positions while specifying a higher price at which you may be okay selling the stock. In my examples, I used option strike prices relatively close to the actual price of the underlying stock and went five to six months out on each strategy.

With the options market as robust as it is, you can choose to increase the strike price as well as shorten or lengthen the time frame, depending on what income level you're looking for as well as your propensity to part with the shares of the underlying stock. For concentrated stock positions, covered calls can be used on just ¼ or ½ of the shares as well, allowing you to always keep a portion of the position.

Now that I've demonstrated two different types of covered call strategies – one using a "dividend superstar" dairy cow investment you may own anyway as part of your portfolio, the other using a low income stock that you may want to own but doesn't fit in anywhere else – I'll summarize the basic rules to follow when looking to implement a covered call strategy.

General rules for covered calls

1. Make sure you would own the stock anyway
   - Good dividend and/or great, stable business model
2. Look at writing calls that expire 4 to 6 months out
   - Should help generate a high enough call premium to make the trade worthwhile
3. Sell covered calls with strike prices that are slightly above where the stock is currently trading
   - Allows some room for appreciation before stock may get called away
   - Allows the investor to walk away with more principal than was invested should the stock get called away
4. Don't be greedy
   - Understand and accept your gains/income are limited

By following these rules, covered calls can be a very effective income creation strategy for every distribution yield-focused portfolio.

CHAPTER 9

How to Allocate Your Portfolio Based on the 5 Components of the Dairy Farmer Approach

I've covered each of the five parts of a distribution yield-focused portfolio: Safe reserve, maturity date controlled fixed income portfolio, dividend superstars, alternative income producers, and high income (but not necessarily high risk). Now we need to look at how much of your overall portfolio assets to commit to each allocation.

Up to this point, I have put a constraint only on the fourth allocation – alternative income producers – limiting that position size to no more than 25% of the five-part total. I would limit the allocation to covered calls to no more than 20% of the overall total.

You may wonder why I'm limiting the two potentially highest yielding parts of your portfolio to smaller allocations. Putting together an entire distribution yield-focused portfolio of just covered calls or high-yielding REITs, BDCs, and MLPs could produce a yield north of 10%. However, it invites unnecessary work, uncertainty, and risk into the investor's life.

MLPs and BDCs, in particular, carry more risk that your typical stock investment. Also, call premiums are very volatile in price and it would be impossible to predict an annual income stream with any certainty using just covered calls.

When creating a retirement paycheck, a level of predictability is necessary to ensure that an investor has regular investment income to support a regular monthly withdrawal from accounts through the distribution yield alone.

The only other requirement would be to allocate at least 5%, but probably no more than 10%, of the overall total to the "safe reserve" portion of your portfolio. Other than that, the percentage allocated to each part of the five-part distribution yield focused portfolio would be up to your required distribution yield (see Chapter 2). This requirement will be based on your risk tolerance, current interest rates, and your outlook on interest rates. Also, consider the amount of purchasing power protection you want to build into your retirement income stream.

The following breakdown for percentage allocation as well as estimated distribution yield may help give you an idea of where to start when allocating your retirement dollars.

1. **Safe reserve:** 5% to 10% of the overall allocation, 0% annual distribution yield
   o At least 5% and no more than 10% of your total retirement dollars
   o If you have a significant qualified as well as non-qualified portfolio, this 5% to 10% needs to be represented in both pools of assets
   o No projected income yield as these assets are designed to basically keep pace with inflation and remain liquid.

2. **Maturity date controlled fixed income portfolio:** 0% to 50% of the overall allocation, yielding 4% to 7% annual distribution yield if built prudently and with diversification
   o If you're completely comfortable with stock market volatility, there's ultimately no reason why fixed income needs to be part of any income investor's portfolio, despite common wisdom.
   o In a low interest rate environment, an investor may be better served by focusing on dividend paying equities,

which may have higher yields and offer the chance of a growing income stream.

o However, opportunities do exist in municipal debt, preferred stocks, and some bonds, and having at least some exposure to fixed income assets can make sense regardless of the interest rate environment.

3. **Dividend superstars:** 25% to 70% of the overall allocation, 3% to 5% annual distribution yield if focusing on dividend sustainability as well as growth

o Since parts 4 and 5 are about stretching for higher yields in non-traditional asset classes, the dividend paying stocks you own in part 3 should be purchased for their stable dividend track records as well as for their dividend- increasing potential. Sometimes this means a stock yielding 2.5% is better than a stock yielding 6%, if the smaller yield means the dividend is more stable and shows a history of consistent growth.

4. **Alternative income producers:** 10% to 25% of the overall allocation, yielding 5% to 8% annual distribution yield if well allocated and balanced between the different entities

o Rather than just load up on BDCs as they often have the highest dividend yields, the investor needs to balance the fourth part of the allocation between REITs, BDCs, and MLPs to have these dollars produce a high, but sustainable, income.

o At least 10% should be allocated to REITs, BDCs, and MLPs, as the diversification offered by these alternative investments (particularly REITs and MLPs) will ultimately help a portfolio (and its income) better weather varied economic environments.

5. **High income (but not necessarily high risk):** 0% to 20% of the overall allocation, 7% to 20% annual distribution yield

o While covered calls certainly aren't required, you're missing out if these aren't a small portion of your distribution yield-focused portfolio. If executed properly and as described in Chapter 8, the downside risks should be no more than those of holding a stock traditionally.

Before I cover specific holdings you could choose to make up these five parts, I want to address the "when" of implementing the distribution yield-focused portfolio.

CHAPTER 10

But I'm Not Retired Yet

The topics I have covered in this book so far should create interest in the prospect of building a sustainable retirement income stream for yourself. Just because retirement isn't immediate (perhaps it's 5 or even 20 years away) don't think that you have to wait to implement the strategies I've outlined.

Implementing a distribution yield-focused strategy years out from retirement can produce even better results and higher income in retirement because of compounding. The dividends and interest being produced before you need them can be automatically (or manually) reinvested into more dairy cow investments. This increases overall income with each passing quarter.

Instead of leaving it up to chance – whether the stock market is high or low – on the day you retire, by focusing on building a sustainable income portfolio as you approach retirement you'll remove the risk of not having enough money to cover your lifestyle because of a market sell-off right before you retire.

It was sad to see retirements get postponed or cancelled altogether because of the market crash of 2008 to 2009. If investors had positioned their portfolios for distribution yield prior to the financial crisis, they would have had an already-established income stream despite the plunge in stock prices.

Growth through income

The peace of mind that comes with having a distribution yield-focused portfolio already constructed before you even retire is invaluable. Don't underestimate the power that dividend and interest compounding can have on the overall distribution yield as well as portfolio growth. Don't think that growth and income are two separate goals or strategies; growth *through* income can be a more stable and effective strategy for achieving your long-term retirement goals.

For example, the S&P 500 index has averaged 9.29% annual returns with dividends included and only 5.11% in annual returns without those dividends since 1929.[17] As these numbers show, dividends, normally thought of as just an ancillary income stream, can have a huge impact on overall total returns.

This effect on returns can be even more striking when seen in the context of an individual dividend paying stock. Over the past 10 years, Procter & Gamble (PG) posted a 126% total return when dividends were included and just 78% without those same dividends.[18]

This is a great difference in total return over a relatively short period of time. In the case of Procter & Gamble, the over-performance achieved through the inclusion of dividends is accentuated as the company makes a habit of increasing the dividend each year.

A dividend yield being further compounded by an increasing dividend amount each year can account for a large amount of the total return an investor will experience. Even for the investor still trying to grow a nest egg, focusing on dividends and, more importantly, on companies that can grow their dividend is paramount to long-term total returns.

Having the dividend payers already in place makes turning on the retirement income spigot much easier. Building a retirement portfolio shouldn't be about suddenly shifting every investment you own from a growth focus to an income focus on the day you retire.

By focusing on distribution yield well before the income is needed, the retired dairy farmer investor need only change the dividend payout option from reinvest to pay in cash, and *voila*, the retirement paycheck is in motion.

That's much easier than scrambling to find appropriate income investments all at once when you're at the mercy of a high or low stock market and a high or low interest rate environment.

In-service distributions

You may be saying, "Yes, I get it. Even though I'm not retired yet, I need to own dairy cow investments now and just reinvest the income they pay out. But the vast majority of my retirement investments are tied up in my company's 401(k), and I can't own any individual stocks in that plan. I only can select from the 12 or so mutual fund choices, none of which focus on distribution yield."

I counter that excuse with a little known strategy called "in-service distributions." Contrary to popular belief, most 401(k) plans allow participants to access their retirement dollars before they retire and while they are still actively employed with the same company.

You're thinking, "Wait, I thought I had to either quit, be fired, retire, or take a loan to get my money out of my 401(k). At a minimum, I'll be taxed and penalized if I pull it out early." Again, the opposite is true if you correctly follow the easy steps to remove your 401(k) dollars using an in-service distribution. An in-service distribution, like a direct rollover, is a tax- and penalty-free transfer of dollars from an employer-sponsored plan that often limits investment choice to an Individual Retirement Account where basically any investment you can think of can be held.

While most 401(k) plans allow some type of in-service distribution option, they will vary as far as the age the participant must be before the option is allowed. Some may allow it as early as age 50, some at age 55, while others may require the participant to be at least age 59 ½. In any case, the process is the same regardless of the age requirement.

You'll need to contact the plan provider or read the Summary Plan Document (SPD) describing the particular provisions of your 401(k) plan to determine the age at which you're eligible to withdraw your funds using an in-service distribution. If you qualify, arrange for an Individual Retirement Account (Traditional IRA) to be opened in your name with the custodian of your choice, and then simply let the plan administrator know that you want to transfer your 401(k) dollars to an IRA via an in-service distribution.

Taxes and early withdrawal penalties will not occur with any part of this transaction. You can just withdraw a portion of the 401(k) dollars, take some now, and then take some later. The plan administrator should be able to communicate your plan's particular rules.

Once the dollars are in the IRA, you can choose to invest in whatever combination of dairy cow investments you want, as outlined in the five parts of the distribution yield-focused portfolio. Just remember: Since you don't need the income, make sure that as much dividend and interest income as possible is reinvested automatically to take advantage of the growth effects of compounding.

If you're not in your 50s, you may not have access to in-service distributions yet. But you may have 401(k) dollars in previous employers' plans. You can move them to an IRA via a direct rollover (again, no taxes or penalty) and implement a yield-driven growth strategy.

It's rare in this day and age for someone to work for the same company for decades. Most workers today will have former company 401(k) assets either still with the old plan or in already established IRAs.

Ensure these dollars do not become part of your current 401(k) plan but get invested through the five-part strategy in a retirement plan like an IRA, which allows much more freedom of investment choice.

There is one scenario where moving 401(k) assets to an IRA may not make sense: when highly appreciated company stock is owned within the plan. Without getting into too much detail, there are special tax advantages that apply to highly appreciated company stock within a 401(k). So, if you hold company stock in a current or previous employer's 401(k) plan, be sure to check with a tax professional before moving these assets to an IRA.

Taking control

Even if you don't have old 401(k) dollars to move and aren't eligible for an in-service distribution, the dairy farmer approach to investing can be put into practice with regular contributions to IRAs or even just a non-qualified brokerage account. In some cases, it can even make sense to reduce pre-tax 401(k) contributions (above the percentage required to earn any employer matching contributions) in order to free up cash for a Roth IRA or Roth Conversion IRA strategy.

You'll need to check with your tax advisor to determine your eligibility for a Roth or Roth Conversion IRA. The point is to use every available avenue to take control of your investments and focus your intended retirement dollars on distribution yield now rather than later.

It can be so important to get an early start on this process so the compounding of returns that dividend-focused investing provides can do the heavy lifting for your portfolio's total return. The only real way to mess up the strategy is by not getting enough dollars invested for distribution yield early enough.

I mentioned earlier that the notion of retirement is changing and more and more "retirees" still work in some capacity to create earned income to help support their lifestyle. For this type of retirement, it's just as critical to put the distribution yield-focused portfolio in place as if the income were required for daily needs. If all or some of the produced yield isn't needed, simply have the income reinvest, compound, and increase your retirement paycheck for when you'll eventually need to tap it.

So, for the "when" part of setting up a distribution yield-focused portfolio using dairy cow type investments, I hope I've dispelled the myth that growth and income are two distinct and separate investment strategies. In and of itself, the compounding of reinvested interest and dividends is a powerful growth strategy that can be used by anyone from age 1 to retirement age and beyond.

> *Don't wait for your growth-focused investments to reach some "magic number" before you turn them over to a distribution yield-focused investment portfolio.*

Compounding of the distribution yield itself can be all the growth you need leading up to your retirement In addition, ihaving a distribution yield established will remove the worry of the stock market declining, bringing down all growth-focused investments with it, and potentially postponing your retirement.

CHAPTER 11

Selecting Investments for the Safe Reserve

Now that the "why," "how," and "when" to invest like a dairy farmer have been covered, let's turn back to our original retirement income and expense example from Chapter 2. I will lay out a specific investment mix (using our five-part strategy) to produce the needed 4.67% distribution yield.

We had fixed income of $40,000 (including Social Security and pension) and $110,000 in total lifestyle expenses. The difference, $70,000, was what we would need the $1,500,000 in retirement-dedicated investments to produce.

If you divide $1,500,000 by $70,000, you get a required yield of 4.67%. If one or more of these numbers seem too high or too low and not applicable to your situation, stay with me. Regardless of your actual numbers, the 4.67% distribution yield should be a good example to work with.

If your particular income and expense numbers warrant a higher distribution yield, don't worry. I will show specific investments that boost the 4.67% yield to over 5.5% and as high as 6% sustainably.

For the purposes of our working example, assume that the above numbers represent those of a married couple named Dan and Sue. Their retirement assets are broken down as follows:

Dan and Sue's Joint Non-Qualified Brokerage Account = $250,000
Dan's Traditional IRA = $500,000

Sue's Traditional IRA = $700,000
Dan's Roth IRA = $25,000
Sue's Roth IRA = $25,000

Dan and Sue also have an adequate cash reserve (checking, savings, money market, and CD) totaling $75,000, allowing all funds listed above to be considered "investable" assets.

This breakdown may not seem like it matters much, since we're ultimately working with the $1,500,000 sum; however, I want to use an account-level breakdown since it's a closer approximation of the reality that many investors will encounter. Rather than just having one large single account, the retirement assets will likely be held in several different accounts, possibly with different ownerships as well as tax rules.

Working with the different-sized accounts in this example will show you the balance required to implement the five-part distribution yield strategy so no particular account is prone to one set of risks.

Dollar amount allocated to the safe reserve

The safe reserve of the distribution yield investment strategy is at least 5% but no more than 10% of the overall portfolio. We *could* take a fixed percentage of each account and allocate that to a safely invested reserve. But when looking at the account breakdown of Dan's and Sue's assets, it makes more sense to use an intuitive approach. For example, the Roth IRA accounts, while nice to have as tax-free retirement assets, aren't large with respect to the overall portfolio; the income produced from them won't be meaningful.

Because they are tax-free, the Roth IRA accounts can be put to better use as a reserve should Dan and Sue need additional resources to cover emergency or one-time expenses. Withdrawing funds from the Roth IRA accounts wouldn't have any impact on Dan and Sue's tax situation. In this case, let's set aside the $25,000 in each Roth IRA account ($50,000 total) as part of the safe reserve.

While you don't have to use Roth IRAs as a "reserve," it can be difficult sometimes to turn small balances into meaningful monthly income. If you do have a larger balance in a Roth IRA account, you can use income-producing investments to produce a monthly stream of tax-free income to supplement other taxable income sources.

Next, we need to make sure we have available dollars in each additional account should Dan or Sue need extra funds, or should dairy cow investments get sick or die. Because tax rules make it very difficult to transfer funds from Dan's IRA to Sue's IRA, it's important to have a safe reserve in Dan's IRA, Sue's IRA, *and* in their joint account.

Moving safe reserve funds from Sue's IRA or Dan's IRA to their joint account to replace dairy cow investments triggers income tax consequences. So, we need to allocate a portion of each account somewhere in the 5 to 10% range to the safe reserve.

Since we have already cut out the $50,000 in Roth IRA assets, we need to be careful not to go over 10% of the total portfolio, or $150,000 in dollar terms. That leaves $100,000 to be positioned as part of the safe reserve among the three remaining accounts.

The following breakdown would be prudent:

Dan and Sue's Joint Non-Qualified Brokerage Account = $250,000
  o   Safe reserve allocation = $20,000 (8% of account)
Dan's Traditional IRA = $500,000
  o   Safe reserve allocation = $30,000 (6% of account)
Sue's Traditional IRA = $700,000
  o   Safe reserve allocation = $42,000 (6% of account)
Dan's Roth IRA = $25,000
  o   Safe reserve allocation = $25,000 (100% of account)
Sue's Roth IRA = $25,000
  o   Safe reserve allocation = $25,000 (100% of account)

Total safe reserve allocation = $142,000 (9.5% of account)

The total safe reserve allocation is near the high end of our range. It gives Dan and Sue a sizable reserve in their joint account and their IRAs. It leaves a tax-free pool of assets on hand should they need to supplement their lifestyle due to unforeseen opportunities or emergencies.

The 8% in the joint non-qualified account, compared to the 6% in each IRA, is intentional. If we need to pull additional lifestyle expenses from the joint account, this action won't trigger ordinary income taxes, which would occur if we pulled money from the IRAs.

We must build unforeseen lifestyle expenses into our retirement income proposition. Liquidating income producing positions creates an income gap, which may lead to more principal liquidations – potentially making the income gap even larger.

Without the safe reserve assets, liquidation of principal can create a death spiral of account depletion that leaves the retiree relying on market growth. Having a safe reserve and building that out intuitively creates pools of money to cover investment mishaps as well as unforeseen expenses. It allows you to focus the rest of your portfolio on distribution yield and avoid depletion of account assets entirely.

Investments for the safe reserve

So, how best to allocate the $142,000 in safe reserve dollars? Remember: Our goal with these dollars is to increase them in a conservative way that keeps pace with inflation. They need to remain liquid as well since they could be called upon at any time as replacement dollars for a dead or dying dairy cow investment or to supplement a retirement lifestyle.

With that mandate, finding suitable investments can prove difficult. The safe reserve represents the smallest portion of actual dollars and makes diversification tedious at best.

Although mutual funds aren't suitable for the other four parts of our distribution yield-focused portfolio, they work well as investments to make up the safe reserve. Mutual funds deliver value for a limited amount of investable dollars. Building out that same number of holdings (sometimes in the hundreds) with such a small dollar amount would be nearly impossible and prohibitively costly in some cases.

While most mutual funds don't perform up to their market benchmarks and are often too costly, there are cases where it makes sense to pay a fee to a mutual fund manager.   These four mutual funds may make sense to hold as safe reserve investment options: First Eagle Global, Ivy Asset Strategy, Permanent Portfolio, and Vanguard Wellington. Their expenses are reasonable for what the fund provides in that management teams have long-term and consistent track records of delivering inflation-beating returns. They minimize volatility of returns, and diversify among multiple asset classes with only a small investment required on your part.

The first two, First Eagle Global and Ivy Asset Strategy, carry sales charges. However, if access to these funds can be gained without paying the sales charges (via the Institutional share class or a cheaply-priced fee-based account), you should consider them, as their management teams are first rate.

The Permanent Portfolio and Vanguard Wellington fund can be accessed without sales charges and are great options. In case you want to consider more options than just these four, or you want to look for additional names that don't carry sales charges, use these criteria when making your selections: a long-tenured manager, a large manager's personal investment in the fund, and expenses that are low compared to similar funds in the same space.[19] (See the box below.) Then, make sure the fund's goal is to deliver long-term consistent returns rather than chase a market benchmark or invest in only a particular sub-type of securities.

What to look for when selecting mutual funds

- Manager experience and tenure
- Manager's personal investment in the fund
- Low expenses compared to peers
- Stated goal in the prospectus should be the same as yours

In addition to the mutual funds listed, consider investments such as higher-yielding money market accounts and short-term

Certificates of Deposit (CDs) (no more than 6 months). Also, look at Short-term Treasury bills, Treasury Inflation Protected Securities (TIPS), and high-grade debt issuances as suitable safe reserve investments.

Treasury bills, TIPS, and other high-grade debt can be purchased through typical brokerage accounts. Treasuries and TIPS are also accessible through direct programs with minimum purchase requirements as low as $100.

With these various options laid out, let's look at an appropriate allocation for Dan and Sue's safe reserve:

$20,000 safe reserve in Dan and Sue's Joint NQ Brokerage account:
- o $8,000 High Yielding (but FDIC-insured) Money Market
- o $12,000 Vanguard Wellington

$30,000 safe reserve in Dan's IRA:
- o $5,000 High Yielding Money Market
- o $25,000 First Eagle Global

$42,000 safe reserve in Sue's IRA:
- o $7,000 High Yielding Money Market
- o $35,000 Vanguard Wellington

$25,000 safe reserve in Dan's Roth IRA (entire account):
- o $25,000 Vanguard Wellington

$25,000 safe reserve in Sue's Roth IRA (entire account):
- o $25,000 First Eagle Global

What's missing

You may be asking, "Where are the treasury bills, TIPS, CDs, or other high-grade bonds?" Because of the current interest rate environment, it's simply not prudent to tie up dollars for months at a time for a few hundredths of a percent in return. When interest rates on CDs, TIPS, and Treasury bills match prevailing inflation rates, they'll be more attractive options. Keep in mind that mutual funds themselves will certainly own these investments.

You may also note the apparent lack of gold or precious metals in the safe reserve. However, First Eagle Global contains significant exposure to gold.

Since our mandate with the safe reserve dollars is to maintain purchasing power by keeping pace or beating the rate of inflation, gold would be considered by most to be worthy of inclusion. With such a small amount of dollars to work with, the ownership of bullion or mining stocks should be left to the mutual fund managers with proven track records of delivering the returns needed to outpace inflation.

Why leave some cash via a money market position in the joint and IRA accounts but fully invest the Roth IRAs? We use Roth IRAs as a reserve for lifestyle expenses. The joint and IRA reserves are needed to replace dairy cow investments. Here, cash makes more sense to hold as a reserve asset for when it may be needed to purchase additional dairy cow investments.

The selected mutual funds are quite good at delivering inflation beating returns over time. But they are not immune from the short-term swings in the markets. They could be down significantly if a 2008 to 2009-type crisis occurs again. In this instance, cash may be the only position without losses.

If capital is needed to replace dairy cow investments, cash would be the first asset in the safe reserve that should be used. This would give the mutual funds time to recover. Also, Dan and Sue have a cash reserve of $75,000, allowing them to use those dollars to cover one-time expenses rather than liquidate Roth IRA investments.

Since the safe reserve is the only part of your portfolio invested for growth, it will make sense to periodically review the investments in the safe reserve portfolio for any necessary adjustment or rebalancing. This means shaving profits from the top performer and reinvesting these proceeds into the under-performer every 12 to 36 months. This rebalancing process is much easier in a tax-deferred account like an IRA where tax consequences do not need to be considered. Transaction costs would need to be factored in if no-load funds aren't used.

It's important to spend time intuitively allocating dollars to the safe reserve and select an investment mix that will allow liquidity as well as achieve an inflation-beating return on average. Mutual funds, while not appropriate for much of a distribution yield-focused approach, can simplify the process of allocating safe reserve dollars.

DISCLOSURE

The investments highlighted in this chapter, the previous chapter, and following chapters are not solicitations to purchase any of the securities or investments. They are not a promise or guarantee of future success from an income or total return standpoint. They are used as illustrations meant to show that a particular distribution yield could have been achieved at that point in time.

Prices, dividends, and yields can all change quickly in a volatile market place. Good investment ideas at one point in time may not be so good only weeks later. Always consult with a professional advisor who can give you specific and detailed investment advice specific to your needs and portfolio.

CHAPTER 12

Selecting Maturity-Date Controlled Fixed-Income Investments

As we get into the next four parts of our portfolio that will produce the income needed to support a retirement lifestyle, it is important to point out that Dan and Sue's distribution yield of 4.67% has changed.

We allocated $142,000 of their $1,500,000 in investable assets to the safe reserve. The $70,000 in income now needs to be produced from just $1,358,000. Dividing $70,000 into $1,358,000 now gives us a target distribution yield of 5.15%. While we don't need to ensure every investment we select yields over 5.15%, it serves as a good target to keep in mind – especially as we construct the fixed income portfolio.

Dan and Sue "get it" when it comes to investing like a dairy farmer. Both are comfortable with fluctuations in the value of their dairy cow investments as long as the income streams remain constant or grow over time. So, they don't mind owning a larger percentage of dividend paying equities since they realize that those are one of the only asset classes that will provide them with a growing income stream to offset inflation.

They know a high-yield bond may look attractive today, but that same payment may not be worth as much in 10 years if inflation continues to increase their cost of living. They want to own some fixed income investments where opportunities exist to hit their target distribution yield or higher.

Dan and Sue's fixed income investments

For illustrative purposes, 20% of Dan's Traditional IRA, 20% of Sue's Traditional IRA, and 20% of their joint non-qualified account will be dedicated to maturity date controlled fixed income. In the IRAs, we'll hold only fixed income investments that produce interest or dividends taxable at ordinary income rates.

Since IRAs are tax-deferred, Dan and Sue will only pay income on these fixed income streams if and when the income is distributed from the account.

In the joint account, tax-free municipal bonds or preferred stocks that get qualified dividend treatment (the dividends are taxed at a 15% instead of ordinary income) will be held. This will reduce the overall tax burden. As non-qualified accounts aren't tax-deferred, Dan and Sue would be taxed on the income produced by the investments whether or not they actually distribute it from the account.

Using 20% of each of the three accounts totals $290,000, or roughly 19.3% of their overall investable total. This is within the constraints we applied to the maturity date controlled fixed income allocation. With these dollars allocated to fixed income, Dan and Sue's accounts can be broken down as follows:

Dan and Sue's Joint Non-Qualified Brokerage Account = $250,000
- o   Safe reserve allocation = $20,000 (8% of account)
- o   **Fixed income allocation = $50,000 (20% of account)**

Dan's Traditional IRA = $500,000
- o   Safe reserve allocation = $30,000 (6% of account)
- o   **Fixed income allocation =$100,000 (20% of account)**

Sue's Traditional IRA = $700,000
- o   Safe reserve allocation = $42,000 (6% of account)
- o   **Fixed income allocation = $140,000 (20% of account)**

Dan's Roth IRA = $25,000
- o   Safe reserve allocation = $25,000 (100% of account)

Sue's Roth IRA = $25,000
- o   Safe reserve allocation = $25,000 (100% of account)

Total safe reserve allocation = $142,000 (9.5% of portfolio)

Total Maturity Date Controlled Fixed Income Allocation = $290,000 (19.3% of portfolio)

Again, there are differences in taxation between IRAs and the joint non-qualified account. (Any money leaving the IRAs is taxed at ordinary income tax rates; money in the non-qualified account can receive the qualified dividend tax rate of 15%.) So, we want to make sure we identify the appropriate account to hold investments based on any tax advantages.

Municipal bonds wouldn't belong anywhere but in the joint non-qualified account. The tax-free interest is in effect forfeited if held in a fully taxable IRA. Also, we want to differentiate our preferred stocks between those that receive the qualified dividend rate and those that wouldn't. Almost any research publication will list whether or not the preferred stock dividend is taxed at ordinary income or at 15%. Taxable bonds and preferred stocks taxed at ordinary income would make sense being held in the IRAs.

Joint account investments

Keeping in mind our limits on any holding of less than 1 to 2% of the overall portfolio size (in Dan and Sue's case, $15,000 to $30,000), for the $50,000 in Dan and Sue's joint non-qualified account, the following holdings will be purchased:

- $10,000 San Jose California Redevelopment Agency bond, 5% coupon, due 8/1/2023
  - o   Current yield = 4.92%, Yield to call = 4.9%, Annual income = $492
- $10,000 Bexar County Texas Hsg Fin Co bond, 5% coupon, due 1/1/2027

- o Current yield = 4.56%, Yield to call = 4.42%, Annual income = $456
- $10,000 Aegon NV preferred stock (AEH), 6.375%, no maturity date, callable 6/15
  - o Current yield = 7.06%, Yield to call = 9.85%, Annual income = $706
- $10,000 Deutsche Bank Capital Funding VI preferred stock (DUA), 6.375%, no maturity date, callable at any time
  - o Current yield = 6.79%, Yield to call = 114.42%, Annual income = $679
- $10,000 HSBC USA Inc floating rate preferred stock (HBA.G), no maturity date, callable at any time
  - o Current yield = 4.79%, Yield to call = 302.86%, Annual income = $479[20]

Total annual income = $2,812

Average yield (income dividend into investment total, $2,812/$50,000) = 5.62%

With our target yield at 5.15%, 5.62% seems like a success. But we're not quite done yet. While the municipal bonds are tax-free, the preferred stock income will get assessed at a 15% tax rate. So, we need to take that 15% off of the preferred stock income total to get a "net" distribution yield picture.

Making that adjustment brings our total joint account income from fixed income down to $2,532.40, or 5.06% as a tax-adjusted yield – not quite the 5.15% needed overall, but not bad in a low interest rate environment. Keep in mind that we still have yet to allocate any money to the higher yielding portions of our portfolio. Any yield near the target distribution rate in fixed income is a success in a low interest rate environment.

Fixed income basics

I want to address some questions that may have arisen as you read the list of the five illustrative investments for Dan and Sue's non-qualified fixed income dollars. Addressing these questions should help you understand some details of fixed income investing in general.

First, why is the current yield higher or lower than the quoted coupon rate? Current yield is a function of the current price (annual income divided by price). So, a fixed income investment trading above its issue price will have a lower current yield than the stated coupon. An investment trading below its issue price will have a higher current yield than its stated coupon.

Second, what is the "yield to call"? All five investments selected for Dan and Sue's joint account can be redeemed by the issuer (called) prior to the actual maturity date. The municipal bonds and Aegon NV preferred stock have fixed dates when this call provision could be exercised while the other two preferred stocks can be called at any time.

The yield to call adjusts the distribution rate to account for the possibility that the investment may get redeemed at a set price (in all cases here, the original issue price is the call price) prior to maturity. For the two bonds trading above their issue price, this would result in a small loss of principal at redemption, thus leading to a lower yield.

With the preferred stocks, the redemption would be above the current price, so the investor would see a gain, increasing the yield. Keep in mind that the call date is important when buying fixed income investments. This will ensure you won't have an unfortunate surprise when your investment gets called. For Dan and Sue, the call dates are well managed to provide a large boost to yield or a small reduction.

Finally, you may have questions on the longer maturities or complete lack of a maturity date in the fixed income allocation. With the low interest rate environment of today's market, especially for investment grade municipal bonds, it's necessary to move further out in maturity to get a higher yield.

Preferred stocks typically are longer-dated or perpetual and the selected three aren't necessarily exceptions. This duration risk is the reason why the maturity date controlled fixed income allocation is limited in size.

Rather than buy longer-dated fixed income issues for yield and take on more interest rate risk (except for the HSBC floating rate that's preferred, where the income will move up with interest rates), it's a good idea to limit fixed income exposure like Dan and Sue and focus more of the portfolio on dividend growing equities.

If you're interested in fixed income, I want to illustrate that even in a lower interest rate environment, it is possible to generate an acceptable yield. However, it may not be *advisable* as that yield will remain largely unchanged until the holdings mature.

Dan and Sue's IRA investments

Now, let's look at the allocation of the fixed income investment dollars set aside in the IRAs of Dan and Sue.

Dan's IRA ($100,000 fixed income allocation):
- $15,000 BellSouth Corp preferred stock (KTBA), 7%, maturing 12/95, not callable
  - Current yield = 6.32%, Annual income = $948
- $15,000 Goldman Sachs Group Floating Rate preferred (GS.A), no maturity date, callable at any time
  - Current yield = 6.28%, Yield to call = 369.64% Annual income = $942
- $15,000 Brazil Gov't bond, 10% coupon, due 1/1/2017
  - Current yield = 10.72%, Annual income = $1,608
- $15,000 Morgan Stanley bond, 6.625% coupon, due 4/1/2018
  - Current yield = 5.22%, Annual income = $783
- $15,000 Nasdaq Omx Group bond, 5.55% coupon, due 1/15/2020
  - Current yield = 4.70%, Annual income = $705
- $15,000 Macys Retail Holdings Inc. bond, 10.25% coupon, due 1/1/2021

- o Current yield = 5.49%, Annual income = $823.50
- $10,000 XI Capital bond, 6.375% coupon, due 11/15/2024
  - o Current yield = 5.08%, Annual income = $508

Total annual income = $6,317.50
Average yield = 6.32%

Sue's IRA ($140,000 fixed income allocation):
- $15,000 May Department Stores preferred stock, 6.25%, maturing 1/32, callable at any time
  - o Current yield = 6.3%, Yield to Call = 30.9%, Annual income = $945
- $15,000 US Cellular preferred stock, 6.375%, maturing 12/33, callable at any time
  - o Current yield = 6.38%, Yield to Call = 34.15%, Annual income = $957
- $15,000 Morgan Stanley Group Floating Rate Preferred, no maturity date, callable at any time
  - o Current yield = 5.59%, Yield to call = 590.89%, Annual income = $838.50
- $15,000 Brazil Gov't bond, 10% coupon, due 1/1/2017
  - o Current yield = 10.72%, Annual income = $1,608
- $15,000 Alcoa Inc. bond, 5.72% coupon, due 2/23/2019
  - o Current yield = 4.05%, Annual income = $607.50
- $15,000 Arcelormittal Sa bond, 9.85% coupon, due 6/1/2019
  - o Current yield = 5.97%, Annual income = $895.50
- $15,000 Anglogold Ashanti Holdings bond, 5.375%, due 4/15/2020
  - o Current yield = 4.63%, Annual income = $694.50
- $15,000 Genworth Financial Inc. bond, 7.625% coupon, due 9/24/2021
  - o Current yield = 6.92%, Annual income = $1,038
- $10,000 Cna Financial Corp. bond, 7.25% coupon, due 11/15/2023
  - o Current yield = 5.33%, Annual income = $533

- $10,000 Aetna Inc. bond, 7.625% coupon, due 8/15/2026
  - Current yield = 5.28%, Annual income = $528

Total annual income = $8,645
Average yield = 6.18%

How to construct your own fixed income allocation

Before I move on, I'd like to make a few more points regarding the fixed income investments selected for Dan and Sue to help in the construction of your own maturity date controlled fixed income allocation. First, besides the Goldman Sachs and Morgan Stanley preferred stocks, all of the preferred stocks and bonds are above investment grade, so we're not taking on "junk bond"-like risk to generate an acceptable distribution yield.

The maturities of the selected bonds are staggered, so Dan and Sue have approximately one bond per year coming due (this is known as "laddering"). This helps the general management of the fixed income allocation. There won't be a large amount of principal returned to Dan and Sue's accounts in any one year that will need to be reinvested. The laddering also helps manage the interest rate risk.

By spreading out the maturities, Dan and Sue will have some principal coming due over the course of the next decade. They may be able to reinvest at a higher yield than the matured bond was paying. This can work the other way as well, with yields falling between now and when the bonds reach maturity.

With this allocation in a low interest rate environment, the odds are Dan and Sue will have an opportunity to reinvest the matured bond proceeds at higher yields. The possibility of reinvesting bond proceeds into higher paying bonds is why the majority of bonds selected for Dan and Sue mature sometime in the next 5 to 10 years. While we want acceptable yields to reach the targeted distribution rate,with interest rates and yields anticipated to increase, we don't want to lock up principal for decades.

When bonds do mature, an ideal strategy would be to cycle those proceeds back into another bond that matches the existing bond ladder. For example, when Dan's Brazilian government bond comes due in 2017, he'll have his other bonds maturing in 1,3,4, and 7 years, respectively. To maximize yield (typically, yields are higher the longer the bond's duration), he could purchase a new bond that matures in either 5,6, or 8 years, so he'll continue to have principal returned to him almost every year.

Each time a bond matures, repeat this process. There are exceptions to this rule such as when an investor can find an extraordinary yield in a short-term bond. In general, continuing a bond ladder in this fashion will lead to higher yields while reducing overall reinvestment and interest rate risk.

You may have noticed that the callable or floating rate preferred stocks offer some great opportunities for a fixed income allocation. The floating rate preferred stocks not only offer an acceptable yield today but will produce more income should interest rates rise. They are one of the few fixed income investments thatmay actually increase a regular income payment (what an investor would see with a common stock that increases its dividend).

The call features also provide a capital appreciation opportunity because Dan and Sue are purchasing the preferred stocks at a discount to their par value. If the preferred stocks do get called by the issuer, then the income stream will disappear as the preferred stock is redeemed for cash. However, they would have much more working capital to now reinvest. If at all possible, try to purchase callable preferred stocks below their par value. This will help boost the current yield and provide a boost in principal should the preferred stock ever get called.

You may have noticed the Brazilian government bond. While developing nations' debt used to be considered a risky asset class, their government balance sheets continue to look much better than their developed counterparts, especially over the past few years. Combine a better looking balance sheet with a bounty of natural resources and open markets, and you likely have a recipe for success when it comes to a five-year investment in that government's bonds.[21]

A higher bond interest rate doesn't necessarily mean a higher risk, either. The higher growth rate in Brazil compared to the U.S. or Europe tends to translate into higher interest rates. Don't look backwards and fret over the numerous catastrophes that have befallen developing nations' debt. Look forward and realize that sovereign debt risks may actually exist in the debt-laden developed nations.

Effect of taxes

Before we get too worked up over the 6%+ distribution yields in the laddered fixed income allocations in Dan and Sue's IRAs, remember that money taken out of IRAs is fully taxable at ordinary income tax rates. So, the $14,962.50 in combined income between the fixed income allocations in Dan's IRA and Sue's IRA is reduced by their average income tax rate. Based on their $40,000 in fixed income and the $70,000 net expected from their retirement investments, Dan and Sue would be firmly in the 25% tax bracket based on today's tax rates.[22]

Because of exemptions, deductions, and the marginality of tax rates (first $17,400 taxed at 10%, next $53,300 at 15%, and so on), Dan and Sue's "average" tax rate may be considerably less than 20%. To be conservative and for illustrative purposes, we'll use 20% as our average tax rate for any of our withdrawals from Dan and Sue's IRAs.

The $14,962.50 total from the fixed income allocations is reduced 20%, yielding net income of $11,970. $11,970 divided into the total allocated to the maturity date controlled fixed income allocations in the IRAs gives us a tax-adjusted yield of 4.99% – not quite the 5.15% overall distribution yield targeted by Dan and Sue, but good for an investment grade fixed income allocation in a low interest rate environment.

Depending on the state of residence, we may need to factor in taxes at the state level as well. However, some states that have an income tax do exempt retirement account distributions. For Dan and Sue, who happen to live in Illinois, this is the case and they won't have to worry about state income tax coming out of their retirement plan distributions.

Between the maturity date controlled fixed income allocations, Dan and Sue have generated $14,502.40 in tax-adjusted net income. With $70,000 being the target (representing a 5.15% distribution yield outside of the safe reserve), let's move on to the dividend-focused equity allocation.

CHAPTER 13

Selecting Dividend Superstars

The dairy farmer investor focuses on creating a sustainable yet growing income stream in retirement. Part 3, otherwise known as the "Dividend Stock Superstars," will be the largest part of the portfolio.

Dan and Sue want to leave room in their portfolio for some alternative income producers as well as covered calls, so what exact percentage should they allocate to dividend growing common stocks?

First, analyze the portfolio at the account level to see what might be most appropriate from a tax and suitability standpoint. While qualified dividends get the preferred 15% tax treatment, Dan and Sue have most of their retirement assets in fully taxable IRAs.

In a perfect world, it would make sense to only hold qualified dividend payers in non-qualified accounts and hold ordinary income investments like bonds in a qualified account. Since Dan and Sue don't live in a perfect world, we'll sacrifice some of the tax advantages of dividends to ensure Dan and Sue hold enough dividend growing stocks to sustain their retirement lifestyle.

With limited access to non-qualified dollars from a tax standpoint, it makes more sense to use these dollars to hold pass-through entities like MLPs or REITs than to hold dividend paying common stocks.

Typically, most of the income generated by MLPs in particular will be shielded from ordinary income tax treatment due to the pass-through of losses, depreciation, and so on. So, for Part 3 of the overall portfolio, we won't allocate any of Dan and Sue's non-qualified joint account, instead leaving these assets to be invested into the tax-advantage alternative income investments previously mentioned.

Next, how much of the IRAs should we allocate to dividend paying stocks? We know that we want to leave some room in the IRAs for alternative income producers (other than MLPs) as well as covered calls, so a good way to determine the percentage of the portfolio dedicated to dividend paying stocks can be to essentially back into the number: 15% of each IRA, $75,000 (Dan's) and $105,000 (Sue's), is appropriate for covered calls, so that's what we'll set aside.

We have already set aside the balance in the joint account of $180,000 to be allocated to alternative income producers. Being mindful not to exceed 20% of the overall portfolio value for that allocation, $60,000 in each IRA brings the total investment in alternative income producers across the portfolio to $300,000, or 20%. The remainder, 39.2%, is left for dividend stock superstars.

With Dan and Sue we determined the percentage allocations for parts 3, 4, and 5 at the same time. Keep in mind, however, that percentage allocations may have to change as you go along constructing your own portfolio. If the yield is too high, consider reducing "riskier" assets like BDCs. If the yield is too low, consider increasing covered call allocations.

The following breakdown is where we now stand with Dan and Sue:

Dan and Sue's Joint Non-Qualified Brokerage Account = $250,000
- o Safe reserve allocation = $20,000 (8% of account)
- o Fixed income allocation = $50,000 (20% of account)
- o **Alternative income producers = $180,000 (72% of account)**

Dan's Traditional IRA = $500,000
- o Safe reserve allocation = $30,000 (6% of account)
- o Fixed income allocation =$100,000 (20% of account)
- o **Dividend Superstars = $235,000 (47% of account)**
- o **Alternative income producers = $60,000 (12% of account)**
- o **High income covered calls = $75,000 (15% of account)**

Sue's Traditional IRA = $700,000
- ○ Safe reserve allocation = $42,000 (6% of account)
- ○ Fixed income allocation = $140,000 (20% of account)
- ○ **Dividend Superstars = $353,000 (50.5% of account)**
- ○ **Alternative income producers = $60,000 (8.5% of account)**
- ○ **High income covered calls = $105,000 (15% of account)**

Dan's Roth IRA = $25,000
- ○ Safe reserve allocation = $25,000 (100% of account)

Sue's Roth IRA = $25,000
- ○ Safe reserve allocation = $25,000 (100% of account)

Total safe reserve allocation = $142,000 (9.5% of portfolio)
Total Maturity Date Controlled Fixed Income Allocation = $290,000 (19.3% of portfolio)
Total Dividend Superstar allocation = $588,000 (39.2% of portfolio)
Total alternative income producers allocation = $300,000 (20% of portfolio)
Total high income (but not "high risk") allocation = $180,000 (12% of portfolio)

Total portfolio = $1,500,000

Asset allocation

We have covered the qualifications and diversification criteria for the dividend paying stocks that we would want to own. With this in mind, along with the overall limits of no more than 2% in a single holding, let's see how Dan and Sue would allocate their "Dividend Superstar" dollars in their IRAs:

Dan's IRA ($235,000 Dividend Superstar allocation):
- $20,000 Procter & Gamble (PG)
  - ○ Current yield = 3.2%, Annual income = $640
- $20,000 Johnson & Johnson (JNJ)

- o Current yield = 3.5%, Annual income = $700
- $20,000 Intel (INTC)
  - o Current yield = 3.2%, Annual income = $640
- $20,000 Abbott Laboratories (ABT)
  - o Current yield = 3.6%, Annual income = $720
- $20,000 Altria Group (MO)
  - o Current yield = 5.5%, Annual income = $1,100
- $20,000 Pepsico (PEP)
  - o Current yield = 3.2%, Annual income = $640
- $15,000 McDonald's (MCD)
  - o Current yield = 2.9%, Annual income = $435
- $20,000 AT&T (T)
  - o Current yield = 5.8%, Annual income = $1,160
- $20,000 Rayonier (RYN)
  - o Current yield = 3.6%, Annual income = $720
- $20,000 Healthcare Services Group (HCSG)
  - o Current yield = 3.5%, Annual income = $700
- $20,000 Encana (ECA)
  - o Current yield = 4%, Annual income = $800
- $20,000 3M (MMM)
  - o Current yield = 2.8%, Annual income = $560

Total annual income = $8,815
Average yield = 3.75%

Sue's IRA ($353,000 Dividend Superstar allocation):
- $30,000 Wal-Mart (WMT)
  - o Current yield = 2.7%, Annual income = $810
- $20,000 Verizon (VZ)
  - o Current yield = 5.5%, Annual income = $1,100
- $20,000 People's United Financial (PBCT)
  - o Current yield = 4.8%, Annual income = $960
- $25,000 Aqua America (WTR)
  - o Current yield = 3%, Annual income = $750
- $25,000 Target (TGT)
  - o Current yield = 2.3%,nnual income = $575

- $25,000 Clorox (CLX)
  - Current yield = 3.5%, Annual income = $875
- $25,000 Landauer (LDR)
  - Current yield = 4%, Annual income = $1,000
- $20,000 Philip Morris Int'l (PM)
  - Current yield = 3.9%, Annual income = $780
- $20,000 Compass Diversified Holdings (CODI)
  - Current yield = 10%, Annual income = $2,000
- $25,000 Waste Management (WM)
  - Current yield = 4.2%, Annual income = $1,050
- $20,000 Coca-Cola (KO)
  - Current yield = 3%, Annual income = $600
- $25,000 Spectra Energy (SE)
  - Current yield = 3.5%, Annual income = $875
- $25,000 Medtronic (MDT)
  - Current yield = 2.5%, Annual income = $625
- $25,000 Hershey (HSY)
  - Current yield = 2.5%, annual income = $625
- $23,000 Becton Dickinson (BDX)
  - Current yield = 2.3%, annual income = $529

[23] [24] [25] [26]

Total annual income = $13,154
Average yield = 3.73%

Between the dividend stock allocations in the IRAs, Dan and Sue are generating $21,969 in annual income (a combined 3.74% yield). Remember, this income is generated in the fully taxable IRA accounts, so we assume a 20% haircut before this income reaches Dan and Sue's checking account.

The 20% reduction means Dan and Sue net $17,575.20. Combining this with the net income from the fixed income allocation, $14,502.40, Dan and Sue now have a total net income of $32,077.60. Almost halfway to their goal of $70,000, Dan and Sue will now use the higher yielding alternative income producer and covered call allocations to generate the remaining income needed.

Caveats

To help with the selection of investments for your own distribution yield-focused portfolio, I'd like to address a few points concerning the "Dividend Superstar" allocation. First, while the 3.74% gross yield is much less than the 5.15% needed, Part 3 of a distribution yield-focused portfolio must have sustainability.

Rather than stretch for yield and concentrate dividend paying selections among only the highest yielding stocks, the allocation needs to be built with an eye towards growth of the dividend income stream. Every stock that you select must have a strong history of maintaining as well as increasing dividends year after year.

You may have noticed the absence of any big pharmaceutical names or major energy companies. While the inclusion of a high dividend stock like Pfizer (PFE) or Eli Lilly (LLY) would boost overall income, it may come at the expense of sustainability and growth.

The increase in competition from companies producing generic drugs coupled with upcoming patent expirations for several blockbuster drugs may create uncertainty in the earnings and cash flows of large pharmaceutical companies.

I may be proven wrong, but I'd much rather take my chances with the companies I recommended, which don't face such major headwinds to increasing dividends each year.

Big energy is hard to include in the "Dividend Superstar" allocation as well because of the costs involved in the energy business and the volatility of prices. The earnings per share of most of the large energy companies are massive numbers when compared to the rest of the market, but by the time those earnings are spent on exploration and development of reserves, there usually isn't much left for shareholders.

Many large energy companies issue debt to raise cash to cover their dividends. On the surface, the earnings per share easily support the per share dividend. After accounting for the money spent to maintain or increase energy reserves, the dividend looks anything but stable. The volatility of energy prices can swing earnings sharply, adding unnecessary risk to the sustainability and growth of a dividend income stream.

The stocks selected for Dan and Sue's IRAs were balanced across the two accounts, an approach that reduces the impact on the Safe Reserve in each account should one industry fall on hard times.

If both Verizon (VZ) and AT&T (T) are held in the same IRA, and the telecom space in general experience dividend reductions, it's easier to manage the event with two Safe Reserves rather than trying to replace both in the same account.

Small intuitive set-up details like this can help with the overall sustainability of any distribution yield-focused portfolio. While producing a current year income is important, it's just as important to ensure that income is there in 5, 10, and 20-plus years in inflation adjusted terms. Individual stock selection through an emphasis on dividend growth is the surest way to achieve this goal.

CHAPTER 14

Selecting Alternative Investments

I described Parts 2 and 3 of the distribution yield-focused portfolio as places where it is dangerous to "reach" for yield. Above anything else, the focus should be on sustainability and growth of the income. Parts 4 and 5, the alternative income producer and covered call allocations, are the portions of the portfolio where investors can achieve high yields to support a higher distribution yield for the entire portfolio.

Selecting the right type of high-yield investments won't add much more risk to the income stream than is present with other investments. While the income yields will be high compared to the dividend paying stocks and fixed income holdings we have already selected, they may be just as sustainable. Especially with MLPs and REITs, it is likely that the current high yield will be coupled with a growing dividend over time as well.

We've already set aside the dollar amounts in Dan and Sue's portfolio for the alternative income producer allocations. Because of the tax consequences involved with MLPs, we'll concentrate MLP exposure in the non-qualified joint account to maximize tax efficiencies as well as avoid issues with Unrelated Taxable Business Income (UBTI).

The BDCs and REITs will be held in the IRAs. The reason why UBTI would discourage an investor from holding MLPs in a qualified account essentially boils down to the forfeit of the tax deferral available within an IRA. If an ordinary income portion dictated by the MLP K-1 tax forms adds up to a UBTI consequence of greater than $1,000, the income should be taxed at ordinary income tax rates rather than be tax deferred– regardless of the fact that the investment is held in an IRA.

Since Dan and Sue will be distributing all of the income produced, this isn't necessarily an issue. But, rather than further complicate taxes as well as give up the tax benefit of pass through losses that MLPs provide in non-qualified accounts, we'll stick with the breakdown mentioned above.

MLPs

So, the holdings for Dan and Sue's joint non-qualified alternative income producer allocation would be as follows:

Non-qualified joint account ($180,000 alternative income producer allocation):
- $20,000 Williams Partners LP (WPZ)
  - Current yield = 5.2%, Annual income = $1,040
- $20,000 Energy Transfer Equity LP (ETE)
  - Current yield = 5.8%, Annual income = $1,160
- $20,000 Vanguard Natural Resources LLC (VNR)
  - Current yield = 8.7%, Annual income = $1,740
- $20,000 Kinder Morgan Energy Partners LP (KMP)
  - Current yield = 5.5%, Annual income = $1,100
- $20,000 CVR Partners LP (UAN)
  - Current yield = 9.3%, Annual income = $1,860
- $20,000 Teekay LNG Partners LP (TGP)
  - Current yield = 6.7%, Annual income = $1,340
- $20,000 MarkWest Energy Partners LP (MWE)
  - Current yield = 5.3%, Annual income = $1,060
- $20,000 Oneok Partners LP (OKS)
  - Current yield = 4.6%, Annual income = $920
- $20,000 Enterprise Product Partners LP (EPD)
  - Current yield = 4.4%, Annual income = $880

Total annual income = $11,100
Average yield = 6.17%

The MLPs listed above have solid track records of providing stable distributions and increasing them over time, similar to the dividend paying stocks we selected in Part 3. It's likely Dan and Sue will see increasing income from the MLPs in their joint account year over year. But, it gets even better for Dan and Sue. Typically, the taxable income portion of the cash distribution from MLPs to the investor is only in the range of 10 to 20%.[27] We'll use 20% to be conservative. So, only 20% of the $11,100 total income will be taxed at Dan and Sue's average ordinary income tax rate of 20%.

20% of $11,100 = $2,220 in taxable income x 20% average tax rate = $444 in taxes due

Dan and Sue's MLP $11,100 income then only needs to be reduced by $444, which gives them $10,656 in net income and a net distribution yield of 5.92% for the MLPs held in their joint account.

You may be asking, "If only 20% or so is taxable, what happens to the other 80%?" The 80% is deemed a return of capital and goes towards reducing the cost basis of the MLP investment. Let's say an MLP was purchased for $20 per share and the first-year distribution amounted to $0.20 in taxable income and $0.80 in return of capital for a $1.00 total. The investor's $20 per share cost basis would drop to $19.20. If and when the investor sells the MLP, taxes would be owed on the difference between the sale price and the now lower cost basis number. Since Dan and Sue don't intend to sell the MLP investments anytime soon, the return of capital acts as a tax-free advantage for current year income.

As I've explained, the disadvantages of later tax filing and additional tax forms complicate the ownership of Master Limited Partnerships, but the unique tax advantages make them an indispensable investment for the distribution yield-focused investor. To ensure you fully comprehend the investment's impact on your situation, discuss MLPS with your tax advisor prior to purchasing them.

REITs and BDCs

The REITs and BDCs selected for Dan and Sue's IRA dollars complete the alternative income producer allocation:

Dan's IRA ($60,000 alternative income producer allocation)
- $30,000 W.P. Carey Global Corporate Property Associates 17 (non-traded REIT)
  - Current yield = 6.5%, Annual income = $1,950
- $15,000 Prospect Capital Corp. (PSEC)
  - Current yield = 12.2%, Annual income = $1,830
- $15,000 Realty Income Corp. (O)
  - Current yield = 5%, Annual income = $750

Total annual income = $4,530
Average yield = 7.55%

Sue's IRA ($60,000 alternative income producer allocation)
- $20,000 Omega Healthcare Investors Inc. (OHI)
  - Current yield = 8.2%, Annual income = $1,640
- $20,000 BlackRock Kelso Capital Corp. (BKCC)
  - Current yield = 11%, Annual income = $2,200
- $20,000 Fifth Street Finance Corp. (FSC)
  - Current yield = 12%, Annual income = $2,400

Total annual income = $6,240
Average yield = 10.4%

Protecting sustainability

I want to point out the account-level positioning of some of the alternative income producers as a way to help protect the sustainability of Dan and Sue's distribution yield-focused portfolio. Since Dan's IRA has a smaller Safe Reserve compared to the Safe Reserve in Sue's IRA ($30,000 versus $42,000), the more predictable and sustainable REIT investments were selected in his account for a majority of the $60,000 allocation.

As an investor, you can reasonably expect both the WP Carey REIT investment and the Realty Income investment to produce a stable and growing stream of dividends long into the future based on their past performance and their business models. So, Dan shouldn't have to worry about replacing either of those anytime soon.

The BDCs (FSC, PSEC, and BKCC) should be sustainable; however, should another severe market dislocation occur similar to 2008-2009, I'm not as comfortable assuming that the high yield dividend will remain stable, much less grow. By splitting up the high-yield BDCs to provide ample Safe Reserve coverage, Dan and Sue have enough current capital in their reserve to replace all three of the BDC investments. There is a big difference in the yield produced by the alternative income producer allocation between Dan's IRA and Sue's IRA, but sustainability of the overall portfolio is improved by positioning the holdings this way.

You may have picked up on the inclusion of a non-traded REIT as opposed to a traded REIT in Dan's allocation. With the downsides listed for non-traded REITs, why would we bother including one here?

W.P. Carey & Co. LLC is an interesting example as the investor has the option of purchasing shares of the company itself (WPC) or purchasing one of the limited partnership REIT portfolios constructed by the company. The decision was very easy for Dan because of the difference in yield between the two.

Due to market appreciation of the WPC shares, the dividend yield is less the 5%; however, the most recent limited partnership W.P. Carey & Co. has constructed (the 17th) yields 6.5%. When you combine this with the fact that the 17th portfolio had purchased real estate assets from 2008 through 2010, it's a safe assumption that the company wasn't overpaying for the properties.

Buying the assets post-crash may allow the non-traded REIT to continually post a higher yield and provide capital appreciation should the commercial real estate market return to more normal levels. Because Dan will immediately take the income from the limited partnership REIT, he won't take advantage of any discount on reinvested dividends for compounding purposes. But this illiquid investment can still be worth holding because of the income yield as well as the timing of the REIT's purchaes.

How to select alternative income producers

- Concentrate MLPs in non-qualified accounts because of their unique taxation.
- Consider the impact of K-1s on your tax filing complexity.
- Know what your REIT owns and how it owns it: triple-net lease, mortgages, retail, healthcare, etc.
- Avoid too many BDCs across one portfolio or account.

Finally, since the investments are held in Dan and Sue's IRAs, we'll need to take out the 20% tax withholding as we have done with the other IRA investments. Reducing the total income produced by the alternative income producer allocation of $10,770 by 20% gives us $8,616 in net income for a net distribution yield of 7.18%.

If we add the $8,616 net amount from the IRAs to the $10,656 in net income produced from the alternative income producer allocation in Dan and Sue's joint account, we get a total net income of $19,272 from just this allocation. Adding this amount to the net income produced from the fixed income and dividend superstar allocations ($32,077.60 total) and we're now looking at $51,349.60 in net distribution yield-driven income.

Without ever having to sell shares of holdings or rely on any market growth, Dan and Sue already have more than $51,000 in net after-tax dollars with which to work with. However, we're not stopping there. The target was $70,000 and we'll rely on the last part of the distribution yield-focused portfolio (covered calls) to make up the remaining difference.

CHAPTER 15

Selecting Covered Calls

You create the "high yield but not high risk" nature of the fifth and last part of a distribution yield-focused portfolio by holding stocks that you would want to hold anyway and using the simplest of option strategies, covered calls, to produce an additional income stream from these stocks. This part of your portfolio can be a perfect place to own dividend-paying stocks that didn't quite make it into your Dividend Superstars allocation.

Maybe the stock's dividend yield was below our 2% threshold or maybe the stock doesn't currently pay a dividend but may in the future. In either case, you can get the best of both worlds by owning the stock as part of your distribution yield-focused portfolio because the covered calls written on the stock will provide the missing income.

In our example with Dan and Sue, we'll do just that. Companies like Microsoft (MSFT) and Chevron (CVX) didn't quite make the Dividend Superstar allocation because of a recent price run-up pushing the yield down in the former and a "big energy" label in the latter. We'll use them to safely produce a large distribution yield to cover Dan and Sue's remaining income gap.

Also, stocks like Schlumberger Ltd. (SLB), Trinity Industries Inc. (TRN), Potash Corp. (POT), and Nike Inc. (NKE) have a history of regularly growing dividends. They would qualify as Dividend Superstars but the dividend yield is less than 2%. You can hold these stocks to produce sizable income streams via covered calls.

For many investors, the most fascinating stock, Apple (AAPL), can now have an appropriate place in an income portfolio and produce a large distribution yield, despite the lack of an established dividend track record.

A covered call involves the purchase a stock and the simultaneous sale of call options on that stock. Since I've already explained the details of covered calls, I won't get into the nitty-gritty of each trade.

For the IRA dollars that Dan and Sue dedicated to a covered call strategy, 6 month forward options will be used and the strike price will be the nearest call option that is just "out of the money." Rather than artificially "juice" the yield by selling covered calls with strike prices below the current stock price, all options used here will be just above the current share price providing a boost to principal should the stock appreciate.

I'll only use dividend income and call premiums to calculate the distribution yield. I won't assume the underlying stock appreciates in anyway, allowing the option to expire and not providing any additional boost to the yield.

Any stock appreciation in our covered call strategy will just be seen as purchasing power protection: Should principal increases result from call option assignment, the now greater proceeds should be reinvested into more covered calls, producing an incrementally higher call premium and an income amount to offset the effects of inflation over time.

Now that we have established that conservative baseline, let's look at the following breakdown for Dan and Sue:

Dan's IRA ($75,000 High Income Covered Calls Allocation):
- $22,000 Schlumberger Ltd. (SLB) covered call strategy
  - Dividend Yield = 1.5%, 6 Month Forward Option Premium = 7%
  - Total Annual Yield = 15.5%, Annual Income = $3,410
- $20,000 Trinity Industries Inc. (TRN) covered call strategy
  - Dividend Yield = 1.2%, 6 Month Forward Option Premium = 8%
  - Total Annual Yield = 17.2%, Annual Income = $3,440
- $22,000 Potash Corp. (POT) covered call strategy

- o Dividend Yield = 1.3%, 6 Month Forward Option Premium = 6.6%
- o Total Annual Yield = 14.5%, Annual Income = $3,190
- $11,000 Chevron Corp. (CVX) covered call strategy
  - o Dividend Yield = 3%, 6 Month Forward Option Premium = 3.8%
  - o Total Annual Yield = 10.6%, Annual Income = $1,166

Total Annual Income = $11,206
Average Yield = 14.9%

Sue's IRA ($105,000 High Income Covered Calls Allocation):
- $60,000 Apple Inc. (AAPL) covered call strategy
  - o Dividend Yield = 2%, 6 Month Forward Option Premium = 9%
  - o Total Annual Yield = 20%, Annual Income = $12,000
- $21,000 Microsoft Corp. (MSFT) covered call strategy
  - o Dividend Yield = 2.7%, 6 Month Forward Option Premium = 6%
  - o Total Annual Yield = 14.7%, Annual Income = $3,087
- $24,000 Nike Inc. (NKE) covered call strategy
  - o Dividend Yield = 1.5%, 6 Month Forward Option Premium = 4.9%
  - o Total Annual Yield = 11.3%, Annual Income = $2,712

Total Annual Income = $17,799
Average Yield = 16.9%

The total income produced from the "Covered Calls" allocation grosses up to $29,005 between Dan and Sue's IRAs. We need to reduce this amount by 20% since the funds come from within the IRA leading to a net of $23,204. Adding $23,204 to the amount previously produced from parts 2, 3, and 4 of the distribution yield focused portfolio ($51,349.60) brings the total amount of net after-tax income to $74,553.60.

With the target of $70,000, Dan and Sue have a sustainable retirement income stream from their assets without having to ever liquidate principal. They have more than $4,000 in reserve income. Although extra income above $70,000 could be distributed and spent by Dan and Sue, it makes more sense to include it as part of a cash reserve in the "Covered Calls" allocation. The $4,000-plus would help in any allocation in the IRA and serve as an additional buffer to the Safe Reserve.

Dan and Sue can also set aside the reserve income to assist with the covered calls. There are a few reasons for this strategy.

First, the covered call stock positions tend to be larger than the rest of the portfolio. The additional reserve will help to protect against a steep decline in the price of one or more of the stocks. The position sizes are larger (particularly in the case of Apple Inc.) due to the nature of covered calls.

Next, since option contracts encompass 100 shares each, an investor wouldn't be able to generate covered call income off of stock positions consisting of just 50 shares. You must own a minimum of 100 shares in order to sell calls against a position. (Note: In early 2013, mini option contracts began trading on a few larger share price securities including Apple. Instead of encompassing 100 shares, the mini options cover only 10 shares of stock. However, since mini options are only available for a few securities at this time, stick with the general 100-share rule.)

With AAPL trading near $600, a 100-share investment unfortunately costs $60,000. While this position in Apple breaks the rule of no more than 2% in any one holding, I wanted to include it as an example of the yield impact covered calls can have as well to show that a stock like Apple can be part of a distribution yield-focused portfolio despite a lack of a history producing income for shareholders.

For Dan and Sue's portfolio, I prefer to stick to the 2% rule and not invest $60,000 in one stock, but, like any rule, there are always exceptions. If you're like Dan and Sue and are insistent on holding a high stock price stock like AAPL in your covered call portfolio, make sure there is ample reserve income as well as a Safe Reserve to cover shortfalls should the stock decline in price.

The other dollar amounts also vary because they represent a round lot share amount (ending in -00) based on stock prices in early 2012. Only one call (representing 100 shares) could be sold on a position of 175 shares. It makes more sense in the "Covered Calls" allocation to use dollars to round up the share amount to an even 200, allowing two calls to be sold, thereby generating double the call premium.

The additional cash will be nice to have around if one of the stocks in the "Covered Calls" allocation falls significantly in price. The cash can be used to purchase additional shares at a lower price, allowing more covered calls, which potentially could produce additional yield. Or, the cash can be used to buy back the call options and close out the position altogether.

Finally, while the calls are sold with the intention of holding them until expiration six months in the future, the price of the calls will typically rise and fall with the price of the underlying stock. Should the stock price fall precipitously, the call option price will also fall, sometimes to the point of being worth only a few cents per share.

At that point, if the investor is confident that the stock price will come back between now and the option expiration, it could make sense to spend a few dollars to close out the option (essentially buying back the previously sold call) to then be able to write more calls on the stock prior to the six-month holding period elapsing. You may not want to get that complicated with your covered calls. However, having additional cash can be invaluable.

Typically, good stock covered call candidates have some type of dividend that is easily covered by great earnings but also may have a bit more volatility due to the nature of their business environment.

Technology and stocks associated with various commodities (like Schlumberger (SLB), Potash Corp. (POT), and Chevron (CVX) illustrated typically are more volatile than consumer- or healthcare-based stocks. Because of this volatility, the price on call options tends to be higher, thus netting a higher call premium and higher yield. While SLB, POT, and CVX are balanced with the likes of MSFT and NKE in Dan and Sue's "Covered Calls" allocation, the additional cash reserve will be good to have should the more volatile stocks experience larger losses in a declining market.

Speaking of volatility, while I don't illustrate it here, covered calls using dividend-paying-gold-miners can offer high yields as well. I mention this because, like Apple, gold is a much-discussed investment as of late and covered calls on gold mining stocks may be an appropriate way to gain exposure while still creating a high yield income stream for the overall portfolio.

For the distribution yield-focused investor, outright gold ownership or exposure to gold mining stocks is difficult as little to no stable income is produced. With gold at record highs, covered calls can be an effective way to gain gold exposure while still helping the overall distribution yield.

Newmont Mining Corp. (NEM), for example, has a 2.6% dividend yield and the six-month forward call options (slightly out of the money) garner a 5.8% premium yield. That totals up to a 14.2% total annual yield, which isn't bad income for the investor looking to gain gold exposure through established mining companies.

If the concept and income potential of covered calls appeal to you, I encourage you to look at options pricing on some of your favorite stocks. You may be interested in aggressive positions like Apple or Newmont Mining Corp., or the more mundane covered calls on a solid dividend grower like Microsoft (MSFT) may be to your liking. Either way, the income-boosting potential is undeniable.

Almost any financial website will have some type of "options chain" that gives you current pricing for the various future months and strike prices. This information can allow you to explore using covered calls on positions already owned in part 3, the 'Dividend Superstars' allocation.

Rather than own shares of the same company in two different places, there is no reason covered calls couldn't be written on each position already held in part 3. While it requires more work, for investors wanting to increase their distribution yield to 6% or even 7%, this would be the easiest and least risky method.

By using covered calls in this manner, risk doesn't necessarily increase and income can be boosted dramatically. The biggest risk is that gains are capped on an appreciating stock. By writing covered calls only on stocks you would want to own anyway, the downside risk of rapid price declines should be minimized, particularly when excess covered call income is produced.

Dan and Sue's scenario demonstrates how to construct a distribution yield focused portfolio – without any tricks or grandiose assumptions of market returns. Any investor can use the simple techniques and risk management guidelines demonstrated here, along with third-party research, to produce successful results, even with little to no previous investment experience.

When properly implemented, the dairy farmer approach to investing for retirement will secure a perpetual source of income and provide peace of mind through the inevitable market ups and downs.

The portfolio was constructed for Dan and Sue's retirement uses actual price and yield data from early 2012 and clearly demonstrates the power of investing like a dairy farmer. At the time, the stock market was pushing multi-year highs, which lowered dividend yields. The prevailing interest rate and bond markets were still historically low with regard to yield.

If Dan and Sue can retire as dairy farmer investors in this environment by relying solely on distribution yield to support their lifestyle, it can work for you in almost any market environment.

Please don't construct your portfolio based on the investments illustrated here and hope for success. Market conditions change quickly. Before you make any decisions about portfolio selections, be sure that the research is up to date and that the latest yield and price data have been gathered. Only you and your advisor will know the optimal mix and selection of individual investments in the current market environment.

CHAPTER 16

Becoming a Better Investor

In this final chapter, I cover the investment products that we didn't choose for Dan and Sue's portfolio as well as the reasons for the omissions. Knowing about these investments and why they weren't selected will help you avoid the many pitfalls that exist with products offered by investment companies. The investment industry is good at creating new products to meet the real or perceived needs of the investing public. As long as there's money to be made by tapping into the investment zeitgeist of a particular time, you can bet that investment products will be developed, whether they're in the best long-term interest of investors.

One example is the preponderance of "technology-focused" mutual funds that emerged in the late 1990s. Launching a new mutual fund focused only on the Internet or on tech darlings in 1999, after the market had experienced a frothy run, wasn't the best idea. Yet, countless offerings emerged that year to capture dollars from investors who believed they had to be in on the craze.

As you can imagine, the funds' returns didn't match expectations. For the mutual fund companies, money had been raised and fees earned, and the failed mutual fund could be merged into another fund or closed. This erases the history of failed returns.

What are the current investor sentiments, real or perceived, that have investment companies scrambling to develop new products to capture investors' dollars? I would list the following as the most important right now by their market segment:

- Generation X and Y
  - o Fees – how to make investing as cheap as possible
  - o Actively-managed mutual funds vs. passive index funds
- Baby Boomers
  - o Income guarantees
  - o Longevity Insurance
  - o High yield investing (with many hidden risks)

Fees

Any investor, whether Gen X, Y, Millennial, or Baby Boomer, should focus on keeping fees low, but this tends to be more of a focus for Generation X and Y investors, who didn't necessarily grow up under the influence of a full-service broker.

Of course, keeping the drag on investments as low as possible means there's that much more money that can compound, and this enhances returns over time. The emergence of the myriad discount brokerage houses (E-trade, Charles Schwab, Scottrade, to name a few) and the ensuing competition for market share has, in general, drastically brought down commission-based fees.

Buy and sell orders can sometimes cost as little as a few dollars or even be free if you use promotional offers or a limited set of particular investments. In contrast, these same buy or sell orders would cost hundreds of dollars via a full-service broker. So, by shopping around a bit, it's very easy for any investor to save on the transactional-based fees, which are public and easy to compare.

Outside of the very visible transaction-based commissions, the fee equation becomes much more complicated. Mutual funds, annuity products, and life insurance products may have "buried" fees. Unless you read the detailed prospectus closely, it's unlikely you would ever know what you were truly paying. Even no-load mutual funds have an internal management expense. Annuities have multiple layers of fees that need to be aggregated, as do life insurance policies that have an investment element to them.

Investment products aren't necessarily bad because they have fees. The products were developed to meet particular needs. In some situations, the fees are worth paying. It's critical that investors start asking the right questions around fees, so they can determine if what they're paying for is truly worth the cost.

Employer-sponsored retirement plans, in particular, have typically been considered the cash cow of the investment industry. Almost every working individual has access to some type of retirement plan and tax deductions and sometimes matching contributions on the employer's behalf encourage investment.

Employer-sponsored retirement plans represent an easy and constant flow of dollars to the investment industry. Many who invest in these plans assume that they're not paying fees. All they know is that when the particular dollar amount leaves their paycheck, the same dollar amount appears in the investments within the retirement account. With no "haircut," commission, or sales charge on those dollars, the assumption is there must not be any fees.

However, this is where the "burying" of fees begins. Each fund-based investment in the account has an expense ratio. Each of those funds also has internal trading costs which aren't represented in the printed expense ratio but are deducted from total returns.

The retirement plan may have a third-party administrator (TPA) that takes a portion of the investment fees. Finally, the plan may have an investment advisor attached to it who also takes a cut of the investment fees. Taken together, these fees can really add up. Even more egregious are the annuity wrappers applied in employer-sponsored plans that can raise the overall fees to more than 2% or 3% while providing little or no value.

The investment companies will reply that these fees are not buried but are clearly disclosed and that investors are able to know exactly what they are paying in a particular account or investment. However, the Department of Labor has drastically changed fee disclosure rules and, beginning in 2012, each employer-sponsored plan statement must list the various levels of fees I just described. If these fees were already being properly disclosed, why the rule change from the Department of Labor?

Fees and the dairy farmer investor

So, how do dairy farmer investors protect their portfolios and negotiate the multiple levels of fees present within various investment products? First, the distribution yield-focused portfolio needs to be implemented in individual accounts like IRAs, where the buried fees found in an employer-sponsored plan can be avoided. Also, if you noticed, Dan and Sue's portfolio didn't include annuities or insurance products. Furthermore, I selected mutual funds only for a very small portion of Dan and Sue's retirement dollars where the diversification of a small amount of money could justify the fees.

The fee discussion should largely be a moot point for the dairy farmer investor using individual bonds in their maturity-date controlled fixed income portfolio as well as individual equities throughout the remainder of the portfolio.

Guess the expense ratio on an individual stock? Zero. The same goes for an individual bond. Call options for covered calls? Again, no expense ratio.

Another very powerful aspect of individual dividend paying/ growing stocks that I haven't directly mentioned yet is the investment efficiency that they provide. Aside from the initial commission to purchase the shares, an investor will never again incur an investment expense or cost. To reiterate, *a stock doesn't have a management fee*. An investor could hold Johnson & Johnson Co. (JNJ) stock for 30 years and never incur an expense drag on the investment. It doesn't get any cheaper than that.

So, the only costs a dairy farmer investor should have to worry about are the transactional-based commissions for buying and selling. Since not a lot of trading is done aside from the covered call portion of the portfolio, these fees should be minimal. Couple this with the fact that an investor today can typically pay very low transactional fees anyway, and you have little to no drag on distribution yield or investment performance.

Active vs. passive management

The fee conversation relates to the debate over active vs. passive management as well. Active management involves the selection of a fund run by a manager who will try to outperform the market by "actively" managing the portfolio of investments. By buying the winners, selling the losers, and timing the market's shifts in sentiment, the active fund manager hopes to deliver value to investors by beating a market index.

For passive funds, a manager may be in charge, but their job is to create a basket of investments that mirrors an overall index or sector. Very little trading is done with the only changes made being to preserve integrity with the index or sector being tracked. The intent isn't to outperform the market index; it's simply to give the investor exposure and mirror the return.

Because of the "lack" of management in the passive index fund, the expenses are usually much lower. Studies have shown time and time again that the majority of actively managed funds do not, in fact, actually beat the returns of their passively managed brethren. So, it doesn't seem like much of a debate.

If passive management is cheaper and leads to better returns a majority of the time, then it must be the better approach. Unfortunately, it isn't that simple. The problem with passive investing doesn't lie with the manager or minimal expenses charged; it lies in the fundamental nature of the indices being mirrored. The S&P 500, the largest and best-tracked index, is a value-weighted index, representing the various values of the 500 individual components (stocks).

Companies valued higher will have a larger share of the index than companies with smaller values. The S&P 500 doesn't simply give each one of the 500 companies included a 1/500th share. A value-weighted index will buy high and sell low as it attempts to replicate the growing values of outperforming companies and underweight the shrinking values of declining companies.

Intuitively, this is the exact opposite of what an investor should be looking for. Chasing winners (stocks that have already appreciated thus giving them higher values) and selling losers (stocks that have already declined in value) is a poor management strategy.

Yet millions of investors who think they've nailed the investment game by focusing on passive management and low fees by investing in an S&P 500 index are just fooling themselves. Any fund that tracks a value-weighted index will own too much of the wrong sector at the wrong time and too little of the undervalued sector that it should probably be buying.

History shows that the S&P 500 owned a huge share of the tech sector in the late 90s, just before the bubble burst. It wasn't the S&P 500 index's fault. It just had to represent the overall market, which had an ever-growing share of tech companies because their values were soaring. The same goes for the financial and energy sectors in 2007.

Active vs. passive management and the dairy farmer investor

With both approaches fundamentally flawed, how does the dairy farmer investor navigate the active vs. passive debate? The discussion is moot.

Avoid *any* management expense and focus on a sustainable and growing income stream aligned with specific income goals. The dairy farmer investor isn't concerned about whether an active or passive approach to money management will lead to market-beating returns.

Research shows that buying and holding individual stocks focused on dividends and dividend growth will dramatically outperform most other investment strategies, but that really is beside the point. Don't obfuscate the purpose of investing by focusing on what will outperform what (active mutual fund or passive index fund) from year to year. The dairy farmer investor simply focuses on building a super-low cost, sustainable, and growing income stream.

Baby boomers

The debates around investment fees as well as active or passive management are issues that affect all investors. They may tend to be a greater focus for the Gen X and Y generations. The investment products developed for income guarantees and high yield income production tend to be solely geared towards the baby boomer generation.

It's no secret that millions upon millions of baby boomers will be retiring over the next few decades and the amount of money that will require management has the investment industry salivating. Tapping into the baby boomer's fear of running out of money, income guarantee annuity products, longevity insurance, and high-income vehicles that carry hidden risks have been developed in recent years.

Annuities

Guaranteed income annuity products are nothing new. Immediate annuities, where a lump sum of money is irrevocably turned into a stream of monthly payments for the duration of one's life, have existed for a long time.

Investors give up access to the lump sum of money through an immediate annuity. As long as the annuity provider stays in business, the investor will never be able to outlive the income stream.

A new twist on this concept provides an income guarantee via an annuity but without giving up access to the principal amount. Essentially, an income guarantee rider is strapped onto a variable annuity product, providing a guaranteed accumulation rate as well as a guaranteed distribution rate.

While the principal invested will move up and down with the underlying investments as part of the variable annuity, a separate number, sometimes called an "income base," will move up at a guaranteed rate. At some point in the future, the investor may choose to take a guaranteed income stream off of the higher of the guaranteed rate or the principal amount while still retaining access to the underlying principal.

The principal will decline with each withdrawal, but even if the annuity contract value goes to zero or negative, as long as the investor follows the rules, the guaranteed income will continue to be paid.

At first glance, it seems like a reasonable deal. A guaranteed income stream can be provided while still allowing access to principal should the investor need a lump sum of money for emergencies or opportunities.

However, there are several disadvantages to this approach. Taking money out of the contract at a rate greater than the allowed 4-7% guaranteed distribution rate will forfeit or change the nature of the annuity contract rider, and reduce any future income payments.

Sometimes, surrender charges may remain on the annuity for 10 to 15 years into the future, making any withdrawals costly. Also by purchasing a single annuity for a guaranteed income, the investor is putting a lot of eggs in one basket based on the financial stability of one insurance company.

Although the guaranteed accumulation rates of 5-8% (not on the principal, remember, but just on the "income base" number) and guaranteed distribution rates typically of 4-7% are attractive, those numbers are based on the annuity provider's ability to properly set aside reserve capital and hedge market risks.

Finally, the layers of fees present in guaranteed annuity products can be staggering. Usually, the aggregate fee will approach 2-4% by the time all investment fees, mortality and expense charges, administration fees, and rider fees are added up. Couple this with the fact that these types of annuity contacts can pay as high as an 8%+ immediate up-front commission to the salesman and you have a large conflict of interest.

Can income guaranteed annuities sometimes make sense to take the place of the maturity date-controlled fixed income allocation in a distribution yield-focused portfolio? Potentially. If the investor has an appropriate time frame, and the prevailing interest rate environment is favorable, the annuity may present a better deal than bonds.

Are annuity products extremely overused by salesmen in the financial industry because of the high up-front commissions? Absolutely.

In general, investors should be extremely skeptical about using any annuity as part of their retirement portfolio.

Annuities and the dairy farmer investor

What is a dairy farmer investor to make of income guarantee annuities? There might be a small role for annuities as a replacement for some of the maturity-date controlled fixed income allocation if interest rates are too low. However, a dairy farmer investor may not want to mess with the layers of fees, contract details, and surrender charges.

The fixed income allocation in Dan and Sue's portfolio demonstrated that even in a low interest rate environment, investors can achieve distribution yields that match or beat many of the income guarantee annuity numbers.

In addition, Dan and Sue will be able to reinvest the maturing bond proceeds in the future into higher yielding fixed income investments should interest rates begin to rise.

With an income guarantee annuity, the distribution rate, while guaranteed, will likely never increase, causing a purchasing power problem in the future. Instead of working with a single annuity provider, dairy farmer investors can maintain control of their money by diversifying among multiple fixed income issuers that provide a comparable interest rate without surrender charges or high fees.

Should you ever be presented with an annuity, one of the first questions you should be asking is, "What is the salesman is getting paid?" You may be shocked when you learn the answer.

Longevity insurance

Longevity insurance, another recent product development, also uses an annuity. The investor sets aside a lump sum of money in an annuity that doesn't pay an income stream until age 85.[28] By having a guaranteed income stream later in life, retirees can spend the rest of their assets and not worry about being destitute.

Longevity insurance is an issue only if you approach investing for retirement in the wrong way – initially focusing on depletion of your investments. Setting aside a large lump sum of money to be used at age 85 or later could be a tremendous waste.

Longevity insurance annuities by rule can't provide a cash surrender value. While beneficiaries may be able to receive the income stream in some reduced form, the cash lump sum is gone forever, even for the initial investor.

Longevity insurance and the dairy farmer investor

The dairy farmer take on longevity insurance should be clear. If you treat investments like dairy cows and focus on distribution yield rather than asset depletion, longevity insurance *via* an annuity would be redundant. Investing like a dairy farmer is its own form of longevity insurance. It doesn't involve purchasing annuities with extra layers of costs or fees. Better yet, it doesn't require giving up control like a longevity insurance contract does.

Closed-end funds

The other big omission from the model distribution yield-focused portfolio for Dan and Sue is the use of closed-end funds. Like a mutual fund, a closed-end fund is a pool of invested assets in which investors can buy shares, to benefit from the diversification of the pooled money. A closed-end fund is different in that the initial pool of money is raised at the outset of the fund and no additional shares can be created – thus the "closed-end" moniker.

When an investor buys shares of a closed-end fund, the process is similar to buying a stock. The transaction is, in fact, a trade of another investor's shares for money. A mutual fund (open-end fund) will create new shares for each investor.

With the closed-end fund, the limited number of shares must pass from one investor to another based on price, which can be above or below the actual net asset value of the fund portfolio. Closed-end funds can be attractive investments for income-oriented investors as they can employ the use of leverage (unlike their open-ended cousins) to increase income yields and returns.

While using leverage in closed-end funds isn't bad for investors in and of itself, it can lead to problems in volatile markets. Leverage uses debt to purchase additional investments. It can be powerful as it can drastically influence rates of return. For example, if you invested $1 and earn 10%, you would have a total of $1.10. If you use leverage, you could double your investment. By using $1 in debt along with your $1 in principal, the same 10% return now results in $0.20, representing a 20% total return on the initial $1 invested.

However, leverage can cut the other way, drastically impairing capital if the investment declines in value. Leverage is debt and carries a cost to borrow. Interest rates are very low right now, so the cost to borrow is very low. This allows closed-end funds to cheaply use leverage to attract investors with very high-income yields.

This approach raises several concerns. First, if a declining market pushes investments down across the board, leverage can cause closed-end funds to drastically decline in net asset value, and losses are amplified. In addition, a closed-end fund may be a forced seller in a bad market. It may have to liquidate good investments at bad prices, to pay down debt levels.[29] Second, if interest rates increase from very low levels, the cost of leverage will increase, possibly leading to decreases in income distributions and impaired returns.

Finally, since a closed-end fund's shares trade through a market rather than through direct investment with the fund, the values can differ wildly from the underlying net asset value of the fund. If investors all want to sell and there aren't enough buyers to support the price, a closed-end fund could trade for any value regardless of how much the portfolio is worth. This dislocation in value can cause unnecessary worry in a volatile market.

Closed-end funds and the dairy farmer investor

While closed-end funds certainly offer attractive distribution yields (sometimes in the double digits), as a dairy farmer investor, you need to approach the investments with caution. Yields may not ultimately be sustainable in the long term. Furthermore, funds of any kind (mutual, closed-end, or otherwise) aren't ideal investments for dairy farmer investors in general.

While they made sense in our example with Dan and Sue for some of the Safe Reserve assets, they wouldn't be appropriate anywhere else. On paper, plenty of funds focus on dividends and dividend growth and may provide acceptable distribution yields. But, they don't focus on a long-term holding period or on providing a growing income stream into the future.Fund and investor goals often don't align.

Expressed fund management fees and hidden trading costs of high portfolio turnover in fund portfolios due to the ever-present attempt to beat the market subtracts from long-term returns. It's hard to benefit from long-term compounding of a growing dividend stream when the fund manager may be changing holdings from one month to the next.

Instead of going after the high yield offered by a closed-end fund or the nice title of a "dividend growth" mutual fund, avoid the management fees and misalignment of goals and focus on building a portfolio of individual dividend payers and growers that will meet your specific retirement goals.

Getting the right help

This book has presented preparing and investing for retirement in a new light and gives you tools to help you take control of your financial situation. You can implement investing like a dairy farmer on your own, without the aid of a professional. However, unless you're 100% confident that you understand the detailed aspects of each strategy presented in this text, consider consulting an accredited financial planner with a strong investment background.

"Wait." you're saying. "You just explained the importance of keeping fees low and avoiding product sales and now you're telling me to consult an advisor?"

While there are plenty of bad financial advisors out there, there are also some very good ones. Good fee-based advisors understand that the fees they charge directly impact the distribution yield and investment performance and understand that they are there to provide advice, not sell products.

They will balance your needs as the client with the need to be compensated for their expertise and intellectual property. A good advisor will also be up-front about fees and should understand the often inverse relationship between fees charged and performance/distribution yield. Don't be bashful about having the fee conversation; this is your retirement.

Ultimately, any advisor you choose will require your confidence and trust. The advisor should demonstrate an understanding of the distribution yield-focused method.

By having a solid understanding of investments, rather than products, your advisor may be able to recommend one or two great dairy cow investments you wouldn't have considered –and this can make up for any fees being charged.

A good advisor should be there to protect you from yourself as well. If your advisor can prevent you from liquidating the wrong investments from the wrong accounts – thereby preventing you from incurring unnecessary taxes – that can easily balance out any financial advising fees as well.

Your advisor can also provide holistic advice on dealing with issues including health care costs, estate planning, and premature death. We're all emotional mammals at our simplest. Having an additional trusted person to consult with before changes take place can make a big difference in the overall success of an investment portfolio. This one last step between you and your money can provide the space necessary to let pragmatism trump fear or greed.

A study conducted by Russell Investments found that an advisor's worth can typically be up to 3.75% annually when dealing with at least a $500,000 portfolio. Most of this worth, not shockingly, is found in preventing bad investor behavior and in introducing tax awareness into portfolio and investment decisions.

Remember: When it comes to your investments, retirement shouldn't be a journey into the unknown. Knowing you can't outlive your money will give you the confidence to draw an income stream from the savings you've worked so hard to accumulate through the years. Retire like a dairy farmer and let the others do the worrying.

ENDNOTES

1   William P. Bengen, Determining Withdrawal Rates Using Historical Data Journal of Financial Planning, October 1994, pp. 14–24.

2   Donna A. Clements, Guide to Social Security, 2010, Mercer LLC.

3   www.ssa.gov

4   http://phx.corporate-ir.net/phoenix.zhtml?c=80574&p=irol-dividends

5   Barclays Capital, US Aggregate Bond Index. Index Products Fact Sheet, April 12 2011. Historical Returns 1976-2010

6   Nouriel Roubini. Nassim Nicholas Taleb "Black Swan"

7   Lauricella, Tom (7 May 2010). "Market Plunge Baffles Wall Street --- Trading Glitch Suspected in 'Mayhem' as Dow Falls Nearly 1,000, Then Bounces". The Wall Street Journal. p. 1.

8   http://www.citigroup.com/citi/fin/div.htm

9   http://www.ge.com/investors/stock_info/dividend_history.html

10 Nasbo. Municipal Bonds in 2011: An Update on State and Local Borrowing

11 Lifetime Income Report: Your Exclusive Dividend Retirement Guide. Jim Nelson. February 2012

12 The 12% Letter. The 10 Best Wealth-Compounding Stocks in America, Tom Dyson, September 2010

13 Procter & Gamble 2011 Annual Report

14 http://www.realtyincome.com/

15 "A Short History of Options" John Emery May 18th 2010 TradingMarkets.com

16 http://www.intc.com/dividends.cfm, February 2012

17 Growth of $100: S&P 500 Returns With and Without Dividends over 80 Years 12/31/29-8/31/2010, Ned Davis Research. Equity Compass Strategies.

18 A Brief History of Procter & Gamble's Returns. The Motley Fool Staff. October 5th, 2011

19 Morningstar FundSpy. Russel Kinnel. 2009 Wiley

20 Forbes/Lehmann, "Income Securities Investor", March 2012

[21]   "Food, Water Shortages Threaten Economic Stability" James Dale Davidson, Financial Intelligence Report, February 2012, Vol. 10, No. 2
[22]   IRS Publication 15 - 2012
[23]   "The Story of Wal-tirement." Dan Ferris. The 12% Letter, January 2012
[24]   "This American Icon Will Make Income Investors Rich in the Next Five Years." Stansberry & Associates. The 12% Letter, January 2012
[25]   "A Great Lesson in the Only Sure Way to Get Rich in Stocks." Stansberry's Investment Advisory, Porter Stansberry. February 2012
[26]   "George W. Bush's Secret Legacy." Stansberry & Associates, The 12% Letter, March 2012
[27]   "Master Limited Partnerships: A Primer" Wachovia Securities 2003, Investopedia
[28]   New! Longevity Insurance for IRAs. Natalie Choate, Morningstar, 3/9/12
[29]   Are These Four Concerns Holding You Back From Closed-End Fund? Mike Taggart, Morningstar, 3/9/12
[30]   How Much is a Financial Advisor's Service Really Worth? Investor's Business Daily, Paul Katzeff, 11/18/16

Made in the USA
Middletown, DE
02 April 2024

52472099R00090